AF725607

Legal, Psychological, & Political Warfare

These eight lessons in legal, psychological, and political warfare were prepared by Commander Rockwell before his assassination. In view of the quality of this course material, it is regrettable that the Commander was unable to complete the entire series of 26 lessons as he planned. The loss of a great leader is a loss indeed.

White Power Publications

Box 21, Reedy, West Virginia 25270 USA

Republished October, 1977 by White Power Publications, Reedy, West Virginia
February, 1985 by Liberty Bell Publications, Reedy, West Virginia
July, 2026 by Liberty Bell Publications, York, South Carolina

ISBN: 978-1-59364-082-8 Softcover

Liberty Bell Publications
655 Sandifer Road
York, SC 29745
1-803-818-5407
dmartyo@protonmail.com

Liberty Bell Publications® is a registered trademark of Liberty Bell Publications LLC, a South Carolina Limited Liability Company.

Printed in the United States of America

Editor's Note

Those who cannot remember the past are condemned to repeat it.
—George Santayana, *The Life of Reason* (1905)

Liberty Bell Publications is reprinting this controversial 1965 book in a more up-to-date style, with enhanced images, a table of contents, and an index. Some spelling and grammatical changes have also been made. No changes have been made to Commander Rockwell's intent or meaning.

These are the first eight lessons of a planned 26-lesson course on the legal, psychological, and political warfare used against Lincoln Rockwell and the American Nazi Party. It is still used to this day against dissidents and, basically, anyone facing the legal system in the United States. Unfortunately, he was unable to complete the full course as planned.

Many of the same issues he warned of have become even more entrenched and extreme since this book was written. It appears, today, that there is no longer a remedy available to this tragic, downward spiral we find ourselves in. Only time will tell if it is even possible with the complete brainwashing we have endured for nearly three-quarters of a century.

Commander Rockwell's love for America and his vision for its great future set him on a determined path to achieve his goals, despite the hardships he faced and the costs, both personal and financial. Our loss of this powerful beacon of hope, at the hands of an assassin, is one of the saddest moments in our history.

Perhaps another will rise to carry the torch as he so boldly did.

This book, along with *This Time The World*, is dedicated to Commander Lincoln Rockwell, with love, in honor of a Great American Hero.

Please send any corrections or ideas to the publisher.

Liberty Bell Publications

Dedication

GEORGE LINCOLN ROCKWELL

Contents

INTRODUCTION

This is NOT a course in methods of outwitting honest police, the FBI, or our courts. We are not criminals; we are patriots—resistance fighters for support of honest government, courts, and police!

Unfortunately, too many young patriots who rush out without thinking the need is to do what they can to stop Jew-Communist treason and race-mixing, find themselves fighting—not the enemy—but policemen! Sometimes the patriots have actually broken the law. In any case, they develop a hatred of "cops," the "fuzz," etc. They permit this hatred to interfere with their efforts to fight the real enemy—the Communist-Zionist Jew traitors and race-mixing agitators. Often, they become almost paranoiac about the "cops," FBI, etc., and see shadows around every corner. By their guilty, sneaky actions, they force the police to conclude that patriots are the very "wild men," "bigots," and criminal men of violence the Jews claim about us.

I have achieved what often appears to be miraculous success against everything the enemy has been able to throw at us in courts and jails over five years now—solely because I have refused to be stampeded into fighting the wrong enemy.

THE REAL ENEMY

The main enemy is the Communist-Zionist, race-mixing Jew! The secondary enemy is the gang of Communist nigger agitators who are working under the direction of these criminal Jews to create riots and bloodshed to start the Communist revolution in America. And finally, at the end of the list, is the savage, stupid mobs of black, jungle animals, now raging and terrorizing White Men and Women in the streets as a result of Jew agitation.

The enemy, the evil Jews and niggers who seek to destroy our great American Constitutional Republic and the White Race which built it, are sneaks, cowards, and weaklings. They can't really fight, except as a pack of jackals or snakes lying in wait. They are not men of real force, as were our warrior ancestors. The only way they can beat us is to get us fighting each other, as they have unfortunately been able to do for centuries. Since they have no real force of their own, the Jews buy it with their gold. With their control of the press, TV, and economy, they get control of White, Christian, sell-out politicians like Johnson and thousands like him in towns and cities all over America.

These politicians control the police departments, and politicians in the Justice Department (like "Bobby," for instance) control the FBI. They then use this control to make honest policemen and FBI agents into troops of the Jewish-Nigger Revolution.

If you allow yourself to be sucked into fighting the policemen, instead of the dirty s.o.b. politicians and Jews who wrongfully and wickedly control them, you play right into the hands of the enemy. You are fighting your own people again!

DO NOT FIGHT THE POLICE

Don't do it—no matter what the provocation! I have come to know hundreds of policemen and FBI agents, many of whom came out like wolves at first to "get me." They are just as easily led to hate us as we hate them, by the Jew liars. But by having iron self-control and being super reasonable with these officers, I have been able to win most of them over and help them understand how foully they are being used by rotten politicians. They may still have to arrest and prosecute me. But there is a hell of a difference when they understand you, like you, and respect you, than when they believe the Jew-lies that you are a crazy, hate-filled criminal, such as they see in the jails all the time. Act like a hood to a cop—and you will be treated like a hood. Act like a just, honest, and fearless patriot, a man with honor, courage, and gentlemanly forbearance, and you will take the politician's soul away from the politicians and Jew liars.

A policeman still must follow orders, however. If the local Jew merchants on Main Street force the mayor in your town to order the police in his force to grab you and prosecute you, the professional policemen will have only two choices, no matter how foul the "charges": (1) he can resign in protest, or (2) he can obey the orders to arrest you and throw you in jail.

FIRST PRINCIPLES

Now, your first principle in learning to survive this kind of rotten "legal" persecution and beat it, year in and year out, is to understand it. Most law enforcement officials know no other way to earn a livelihood, and usually have families and kids to support. When faced with resigning to save you, or carrying out their orders, most of them will go all the way to save their jobs, short of perjury. And you can't really blame them too much. If any cop did resign, another would take his place, perhaps a Jew or nigger. And so you can expect that good policemen will often arrest and jail you.

But you must start right now to make yourself understand, in your heart, that the policeman is not the enemy (unless he actually beats you, etc.—which he is not required to do). I have come close to beatings several times, particularly in Southern jails where the jailers actually believed I was a Communist race-mixer, believe it or not, but I have never yet gotten a beating by a cop!

I repeat, Principle One is: Do not get sucked into fighting the cops!

This course will teach you your rights and to respect the law and the system set up for justice in America. A huge man attacked by a baby does not get hysterical and lash out at the baby, or any number of babies. When you know what you are doing and are absolutely sure of yourself and your rights, you will feel sorry for unprofessional and stupid police officers who try to horrify you, scare you, and bully you. And your attitude of quiet, professional competence in the presence of unprofessional policemen will make them feel crushingly inferior and wrong and take all the fight out of them. I have found that only Jew cops will be able to stand up to quiet professionalism. Even nigger cops can't keep up the bully act when you rise above it and show no fear or hatred. Jews, of course, full of insane paranoia, will often threaten you with death and have even pulled their pistols on us in jail cells. But they are usually too chicken to do anything, and you should laugh at such utter cowards. Laughter utterly crushes these Jew terrorists and bullies.

Policemen, being mostly clean-cut men of force, are spiritually on our side, not the side of Jew-Communist cowards, sneaks, weaklings, and rats. In their hearts, most of them roundly hate the Jews, niggers, Communists, beatniks, etc. In big cities, cops have "had it" with niggers, up to "here"! I have never found a security section of a big city police department with a Jew in it. Most of them are patriotic Irishmen who "know the score." And I have yet to meet a Jew FBI agent.

To sum up Point One of this course—Do not fight the cops! Stand up to bullying, of course, and defy illegal harassment. But go as far as possible to make the average cop like you and respect you—and make him hate the political bosses who force him to persecute you—not hate you!

You did not take this course and pay $85 to read a lot of soft soap, but to enable you to win political victories, to lead. I will not write what some may want to hear, but what you must hear to win.

The courts are not all Communist-controlled, as it once seemed to me before I started fighting and learned first hand why the Reds, Jews, and niggers so often win in the courts.

The Jews do their homework; they prepare their cases and they do a magnificent job of presentation in the courts. They work hard. Time after time, I have seen our side, soft and flabby from decades of domination, just trusting that the old ways would get them by in court. Our side has never yet, for instance, presented the kind of smashing, unbeatable, factual case on the inferiority of the niggers we could present if our side spent money, time, and effort on such research and court work as do the Jews.

In short, many of the court victories which seem, from the outside, to be the result of Communist and nigger-loving judges, are the result of a good case presented before the judge by the Jews—and no real case at all for our side. If you were the judge in that court, sworn to decide the case on the basis of what was presented to you, you would have little choice but to go along with the Jews and race-mixers, because they often have the only real case.

This is not to say there aren't plenty of rotten Jew, nigger, and Communist judges. We have suffered from them brutally.

But the fact is that the majority of the judges are relatively fair. If that were not the case, I would not be sending this course to you through the U.S. mail, and you would not be reading it. We would all be in jail—where the Jews would like to throw us and would if they could! But time after time, when we fight hard, honest judges have defied the Jews and granted us our rights, even though they were begrudged.

In short, you can win in the courts—as I have won the right to speak in Union Square, New York, even from our awful Supreme Court.

RESPECT FOR THE LAW!

This whole course, from beginning to end, is based on absolute respect for the law, for the courts that administer that law, and for the policemen who enforce the judgments of the courts.

Our kind of law is something sacred to me. The law should be sacred to all White, Christian patriots, because it is solely the product of the White Race. All over the world, all through history right up until today, the dark races have tyrannized each other, sold each other into slavery, and generally acted like beasts to each other. Only the Western White Man developed a concept of not pushing around little guys and protecting the "rights" of those who cannot protect themselves from the State. The so-called Jewish religion is full of dark, bloody, and vengeful tyranny, and the dark races of the world in Asia, Africa, and South America practice the most unspeakable brutality and bullying against those who fall into their power. Only in the White, Christian West have we developed a concept of real, objective justice. That White concept of "justice" is a sacred thing to me. It is what I am fighting for, and what I presume you are fighting for.

We cannot and must not destroy that holy, White Man's gift, which is now exemplified in our courts and judicial system. We must, of course, destroy the rottenness in the courts, and run nigger revolutionists posing as judges and

Jew tyrants off the bench. But the system of justice we have, while it has faults, is the best in the world so far. It is solely responsible for our survival today. Without our system, we would long ago have been thrown into the Jewish dungeons.

So I therefore start this course off with the admonition to treasure our system of courts, even if you wind up being persecuted and tortured by some vile Jew or nigger or Shabaz-Goy judge.

We are the forces of order, of law, of civilization, of decency, and wholesomeness.

The enemy hates our people, our race, our system of government, and the courts we have set up. He is using those courts to destroy the race that alone can maintain the courts.

Our job is not to fight policemen or courts, but the enemy who is out to destroy these things.

If a rotten cop or a rotten judge happens to get his filthy hooks on you—fight! Fight the injustice, and that particular cop, or that particular judge. But never let the persecution and injustice goad you into hating your own—hating Anglo-Saxon justice and the system set up by our inspired Founding Fathers to protect the innocent and the individual from tyrants and injustice.

The twenty-six lessons that follow will be solidly based on that concept, and it is vitally important that you understand the principle involved here, not only in your mind, but in your heart.

The end result will be that you will become an ally of good law-enforcement officers and honest judges in protecting our race and nation from the Communist-Jew-nigger assault now taking place.

☆ ☆ ☆

Students must clearly understand that no "course," written in advance of a particular situation, can be used as an absolute rule of what to do in that particular situation.

The advice and suggestions you will get in this course are the best I know in MOST situations we have faced in more than five years of desperate and successful battling the enemy from the gutters to the TV screen and all the way into the Courts. But there are bound to be situations where these suggestions do not apply. There are bound to be State laws that do not "fit" these suggestions and generalizations. There are bound to be atypical officials and judges. In short, there are endless possibilities where you will have to use wise and mature judgment in applying these basic suggestions, or you will not succeed.

But that is true of ANY course or set of rules. He who slavishly applies the same rule, every time, to all situations without wise, personal judgment, is doomed to sure catastrophe sooner or later.

Therefore, students are warned to THINK for themselves. You will be better off at least KNOWING these rules than not knowing them. You will be still better off knowing not only when and how to apply them, but when and how NOT to apply them in special situations. This course does not pretend that you can or should dispense with a good, professional, and honest attorney. On the contrary. If you can find a good one and a fearless one, by all means, hire him if you can. But most of us are usually too poor to afford the kind of legal help the Jews can usually afford, and wind up with no lawyer, on our own resources. In such circumstances, this course may save your life. But we cannot take the responsibility for the final judgment of what YOU should do in any particular situation. It will be YOUR life or liberty in the balance, and final decisions will be YOURS. You will find this course a tremendous help in making those life-and-death decisions, but it cannot take the place of a fine, professional attorney when you can get one.

If you follow the rules and principles laid down in these lessons, you will someday find most of the policemen in your area coming to you in friendship and with the utmost respect. You will never again fear or run away from cops. And you will know exactly how to deal with a rotten cop or a rotten judge. Instead of you fearing them—they will fear you

A FINAL NOTE ON SECURITY. . . .

Much of the effectiveness of this course will be lost if it is compromised. There is nothing illegal or improper in the lessons. But there are vital elements in strategy that I have divulged to our students. If the Jews or other hostile elements know the contents of this course, it will make it far more difficult for all of us to keep beating their standard methods of illegal persecution, and it will make the propaganda approaches we teach far less powerful.

The course costs MONEY, which I believe will keep the Jews from having one of their stooges enroll. They just can't bear to pay out that Jewish gelt to help us, even to find out what we are doing.

Therefore, please guard this course as one of your most valuable private documents. It will very probably save your liberty some day, and possibly your life. But not if you permit it to fall into other hands. Trust no one with it, except those you are absolutely sure of. And remember that some you feel "sure" of today, may turn rat tomorrow. It has happened to us here a hundred times.

LESSON NO. 1
Basic Criminal Law

First Principle: Do Not Break the Law!

This principle is not intended to mean that you will never be charged with breaking the law. If you stand up to the Jew-Communist-Nigger hell-raising, tearing up America, you will wind up not only charged, but sometimes in jail, in spite of all innocence.

It also does not mean you should be afraid to picket, speak, or otherwise stand up legally to oppose treason and racial ruination, even if told these things are "illegal." I myself have been arrested and jailed many times for these things. Local areas, especially in the South, often have unconstitutional and illegal restrictions, and you will usually be too poor or too hard-pressed to challenge such illegal restrictions.

Nor does this principle of never breaking the law mean that you should sit idly by while some Jew or nigger viciously insults our Republic, our religion, our flag, our women, or our race. More and more, these arrogant Communists and rats are actually doing these things; and I am not ashamed to admit that no decent American is so afraid of an assault charge that he will permit such intolerable insults and attacks on our holiest traditions, institutions, and especially our women. When such things happen, our men often are unable to control themselves, and it is worth any jail time we have to do to stand up for our country and our race against traitors. But I advise maximum self-control, even in these cases. My point here is only that I cannot help respect a man who goes after the scum who haul down our flag, as they did in San Francisco last week, or grab our women, or boast how they laugh to see American pilots shot down over Viet Nam, as some of the Cuba traitors did in Congress.

To get down to brass tacks—let's suppose you have tried to pass out some literature or picket or otherwise exercise your rights under the First Amendment to the U.S. Constitution. In spite of the fact that niggers are tearing up the town, there is a good chance they will nevertheless arrest you for daring to oppose the general hell. Often, the cops' theory is that it is bad enough they have to have the uproar from the niggers, who are backed all the way to the White House. But it is too much that you should get out there too to oppose the Jews, and you are not backed by any White House. So they pinch you. What should you do?

The first thing to do if you are stopped by a policeman is to be sure he is a policeman. Sometimes, we have been stopped and buffaloed by Jews trying to give the impression they are cops in plain clothes. So if somebody comes up to you representing himself to be a detective, you have an absolute right to see his badge or papers, and if he fails to show them to you, you have the further right and even the duty to refuse to go along with him in any way, and to use physical force to resist, if necessary. This right, of course, should be used very judiciously, but you must also be on your guard against kidnappers pretending to be police officers. It has happened. Your only protection is the fact that the officer must show you a badge or certificate of his authority to interfere with your liberty in any way.

If the officer is in uniform, note and remember his badge number. That's vitally important. If there are irregularities later, as often happens, you can take proper action only if you know "who did it."

Next is the question of whether you are "under arrest" or not. If you are not placed under arrest, you have no duty whatsoever to go anywhere with an officer. If he asks you to "come along" or "let's go downtown," etc., you must ask, "Am I under arrest?" If he replies that you are not, but that "you'd better go along," then you must use your judgment whether or not to comply. In most cases, I recommend that you do cooperate, unless there is a very obvious frame-up and attitude of vicious hostility. In that case, insist that you be placed under arrest before you go along.

The moment you are placed under arrest, you have a right to be informed on what grounds. If not told, you must ask, clearly, courteously, and firmly. Insist on being told what for.

Never get maneuvered into a "sloppy" legal position if the officer appears vicious and mean. Have the officer place you under arrest and tell you what for, making sure to note his badge number.

Your attitude must never be fearful, cringing, or defiant. It is just as bad to be arrogant and defiant as to cringe. Every dirty, criminal hood a cop sees is snotty and "hoody," pretending he is so brave he defies all cops, etc. If you act like a hood, you will be treated like a hood. If the police try to bully you, maintain a patient attitude as though you were actually the Governor of the State, whom they didn't recognize, and you were waiting confidently for these stupid, oafish louts to be told the facts, and that you are far, far above their cheap terrorism. If they try the terror bit, do not get emotionally involved with them. Remain calm, aloof, confident, and firm. It sometimes helps to point out that you know the law and how to file civil suits (when that is the truth—don't bluff) and that their fun with you now is going to cost them dearly, in cash, later. But don't throw that at them as a threat, simply as a calm statement of fact. The object is to make them feel rotten inside, which you can do. Usually, they will slink away with their tails between their legs. If you curse them and try to fight back, they will have a ball with you and get their fighting blood up. Usually, only Jew cops will actually beat you when you are absolutely helpless and not defying them. I have been spared this, so far, but we have found there is only one answer to Jew cops who try terror, and that is to laugh when they threaten. Never give these Jew bullies the satisfaction of showing fear.

Upon arrival at a police station, you will be "booked"—your arrest will be "logged."

In most cases, at that time, you have the right to have your bail set. And, except in capital and very unusual circumstances, you have an absolute right to bail.

In cities like Philadelphia and New York, they usually set our bail at ten or fifteen thousand dollars, even for disorderly conduct, although that is more than they ask for robbery and assault.

If they do set exorbitant bail to harass and hurt you unfairly (as many Jew judges almost always do), you can and must ask the court at the first hearing you get to reduce your bail and be sure your request is made a matter of record. If they deny it, you should appeal to the next higher court, and it will usually be granted, even in New York (but not Philadelphia).

At the "booking," you must also insist, firmly and courteously, on being officially informed in writing of the charges.

There are two kinds of charges: misdemeanors and felonies.

Misdemeanors are relatively minor offenses, such as disorderly conduct. They are never punishable by more than a year. Anything punishable by more than a year in a penitentiary is a felony.

If you are charged with a misdemeanor, you will have to judge, by the circumstances, whether or not to "talk," to discuss the affair with the police or others. You can usually tell if the arrest is minor and was just to get you "off the street," in which case your best bet is to be as friendly and decent to the police officers as possible, since they are usually only following orders.

If you are charged with a serious offense—a felony—under no circumstances should you so much as open your mouth to anybody about the case while in custody! Nobody! Not one word! Not in your cell! Not even to some lawyer who may arrive and say he's been appointed to help you. In Philadelphia, one of our men was approached by just such a Jew lawyer with offers of help, while he was in jail, and the offers were 1000% phony and designed to trap our boy into pleading "guilty" to what he claimed were "lesser charges"—when our boy was guilty of nothing.

Don't talk to fellow prisoners about the case. I repeat, if charged with a felony, talk to no one about the case, no matter how friendly he may seem. Prisoners may be phony, and cells may be bugged.

To all demands that you talk, reply, "I will be glad to accept all questions in writing through my attorney." If they press you intolerably, repeat that same statement over and over until they are as tired of it as you are. They will never stop as long as they think you will "break." So make them see at the beginning that you will never change, and you will save all hands a lot of trouble.

Watch out for "two-way" mirrors in interrogation rooms and never fool around with any papers on desks in detectives' offices if you are left alone. Do not even take a "peek" at anything, since they sometimes leave phony "orders," etc., there to horrify you.

Beware of the "good-guy-bad-guy" technique.

When they have a "green" catch, unscrupulous detectives will sometimes assign two men to interrogate you. One of the men will stay sort of quiet, while the other is absolutely vile to you. The "bad guy" will bully, shout, perhaps curse you, deny you water or any comfort, etc., and generally do all he can to make you really HATE him. He knows very well you're not going to talk to him. His job is to get you emotional; get you hating him with a red-hot passion. The other guy, the "good guy," will look disgusted while this is going on, try to convince you he wants to make the bully stop, and will often get into a near fight with the "bad guy" trying to "protect" you.

After the "bad guy" has rampaged around enough to get you good and sore, and the "good guy" has you convinced he is your friend and is doing his best to stop this other cop, the "bad guy" will stomp out in a rage, cursing that he has "failed."

As soon as he is out of the room, the "good guy" confides to you how the whole police department despises the "bad guy," and he apologizes for the brow-beating, etc.

You can't help but appreciate the "good guy" after a dose of the "bad guy." The good guy gives you a cigarette, water, and sympathy. Before you know it, you are talking to the "good guy"—just as they planned it!

I repeat, if they charge you with a serious offense, don't talk, not to "bad guys," and not to "good guys"!

Do not protest your innocence, tempting as it may be. Just say nothing.

In any case, unless there is some political reason for remaining in jail, you should do everything possible to get put on bail—not just because jail is rotten, but because you have a far, far better chance of winning any criminal case if you don't look like a criminal. And when you are dragged into court in chains, you are half convicted by appearance. You should walk in there like a gentleman, always well-dressed and always quiet and well-behaved. Never, never go into a court for a trial dressed in anything else but a suit, and a well-pressed, reserved suit at that. No sweaters or sweatshirts, T-shirts, Hawaiian shirts, dungarees, etc.

Most bondsmen are Jews with some niggers, especially in big cities. But do not despair of getting bail from these Chosen Ones. True to their natures, some Jews would bail out Adolf Hitler for a buck. Try them all—we have almost always found at least one—often black!

If possible, try to put up cash bail with the court, if permitted. That will save a lot of money if bail is high, since you will get almost all of it back.

If held in jail, you have the right to at least one phone call.

There will usually be either a trial or a hearing the following day, depending on whether the charge is minor or serious. Serious cases require a sort of miniature trial within hours of your arrest. The very excellent theory is that no police officer has the right to deprive you of your liberty, even to hold you for trial, and that only a judge or magistrate can decide whether to admit you to jail, and judge whether there are enough grounds to hold you for trial.

Therefore, before going into details of a trial proper, I will cover what you should and must do at a "hearing" on a serious offense.

(1) If you are not yet sufficiently familiar with the law to defend yourself at the hearing, or if the charges are very serious, you should insist on a lawyer before anything else. Recent Supreme Court decisions have granted you the absolute right to a lawyer at every step of the proceedings in serious cases, and you must insist on that right, or they may rule that you waived it later. If you are too poor to pay a lawyer, they've got to give you one. But be careful. These "drunk tank" lawyers, usually assigned to such cases, are often utterly unsuccessful lawyers who hang around the courts for a few free "handout" cases from which they hope to pick up a fee. Once in a while, you will find a really good one. But I have often found horrible ones who won't fight and couldn't fight if they wanted to. Remember, anything your lawyer says in court commits you; it's the same as though you said the things yourself. If your lawyer is not really fighting and is selling you out, you must discharge him on the spot. If you do not, you can't complain later in jail. You are presumed to approve every word he says. Do it diplomatically, if you can. Ask him privately to ask the judge to excuse him. If he won't, stand up and demand that you be allowed to defend yourself. Further, especially in small towns, you may run into what I call "the courthouse gang"—an informal sort of exclusive social and professional "club" consisting of the judges, the top police officials, the sheriff, the prosecutors, and the defense attorneys—who put on a good show of fighting in public, but do most of their work in friendly "conference." In such a set-up, you may find yourself the "bargaining point" in various "deals," all of which dump you in the state can. In spite of all this, if the charges are extremely serious, involving five or more years in the penitentiary, you almost must have a lawyer. An extremely effective system I have discovered, when there are two or more of you on trial for the same offense, as usually happens, is for the defendant who knows the law best to go without a lawyer, while the others insist on one. That way, you get the benefit of the lawyers, but you also protect yourself from sell-out by retaining the right to address the court and jury yourself and add your political knowledge into the balance.

(2) If the offense is serious, and especially if you have no lawyer, insist on a court reporter—a stenographer to take down every word. This is your only real protection against a vile, bullying judge. And it really works. Judges don't dare get too vile, when it's all a matter of written record.

(3) If there has been any brutality or irregularity in the arrest, booking, bailing, or jailing, now's the time to squawk. If you don't, they will claim it didn't happen, or you lost the right, etc. If a Jew cop pulled a gun on you in a cell, as has happened to us in Philadelphia and New York, report all circumstances and his badge number the minute you get before a judge.

(4) If your bail is too high, ask for it to be reduced in open court.

(5) At the hearing, they usually will "arraign" you. If you have no lawyer, you will have to go through this all by yourself. It means they stand you up and tell you what you are supposed to have done wrong, and you are supposed to tell them how you stand on the affair.

If the offense is serious, always, always, always plead "Not Guilty!"

Do not listen to deals, arrangements, threats, or offers of any kind. Plead "Not Guilty!"

You also have the right to "stand mute" (to say nothing), or to plead "nolo contendere."

If you "stand mute," the court will take it as a "not guilty" plea.

If you plead "nolo contendere," it means you answer, but won't fight.

Again, plead "Not Guilty!"

The only exceptions are minor offenses, where you are guilty of losing your head for a moment, for instance, and bopping some nigger Communist hauling down the American flag, etc. Here, it is better to plead guilty as soon as possible and forfeit minor collateral or, if permitted, a fine.

Let me repeat, do not listen to "deals," offers, or threats from any officials while you are in jail. When you are out, you may be interested in some of the deals to "get out of town," even though not guilty, because you are too poor or pressed for time to stay and fight, and can afford to stay out of that town anyway. But in jail, especially in Red, Jew cities like Philadelphia, you will almost always be told that your buddies have all "ratted" on you, the Party has deserted you, your companions have all accepted the deal, etc. You will also be told that the alternative to their rotten "deals" is "twenty years," etc., etc., etc. They actually do this in New York, Philly, etc. And the one who does it is usually the "Public Defender" they send to "help" you. I repeat, do not make deals in jails. You can only lose.

Remember that you will be somewhat "shook up," to say the least, in jail, especially if it is your first time. I am only being honest. You will probably be frightened if they are threatening you with "big time." So don't listen to any of their "news" about how your buddies have ratted and deserted you and you are the "sucker," etc. And don't make deals!

After you have been arrested, booked, allowed bail, or jailed, arraigned, and given a hearing, you will be ready for trial.

I cannot emphasize often enough that you should work hard if you are facing a trial without a lawyer, and even with a lawyer (unless you know for sure that he is a good lawyer).

Go to the nearest law library and start studying. Here's how: Find a set of books called *Corpus Juris Secundum* and/or *American Jurisprudence*. Look up the crime with which you are charged. There will be a long and detailed article on it. Study it—and then follow up on all cross-references. Then get the official statutes, the laws under which you are specifically charged. Get an "annotated" edition of the laws, and you will find, under the heading of your charge, many previous cases that have been tried and decided, with all the fine points involved. Follow up on all of these in the various "Reports." (You'll have to ask the librarian for help on this until you learn how to find them.)

Check the charges against you to see if they actually charge a crime. For instance, if it is alleged that you were "disorderly" in that you "publicly read a copy of *Mein Kampf* (to exaggerate for illustration), there is no crime alleged. You'd be surprised how often the charges are sloppy and do not allege a crime. A crime must be illegal by "common law" (long tradition) or by a specific statute. If they allege a specific statute, they are required to be very, very accurate in every detail. Catch a serious omission, and you've got 'em. If you find there is anything at all wrong with the charges, make a "motion" to the court to have the charges dismissed on the grounds that they do not satisfactorily allege a crime, etc. Here's the rough form for such a motion:

COMMONWEALTH OF VIRGINIA

IN THE CIRCUIT COURT OF ARLINGTON COUNTY

Commonwealth,	)	
	)	
Plaintiff	)	
	)	
vs.	)	Case No.________
	)	
(Your name),	)	
	)	
Defendant	)	

MOTION TO DISMISS

COMES NOW THE DEFENDANT in the above entitled Cause, and moves the Honorable Court to dismiss the charges against him and, for his reasons, states that;

1. (Here write that the charge fails to state a crime or whatever other reason you have.)

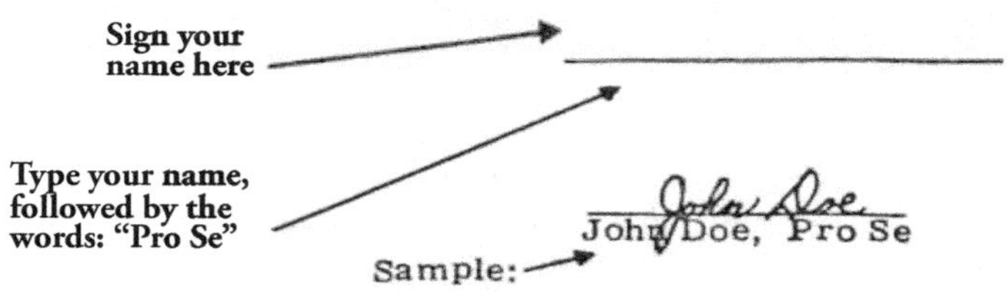

You should also ensure that the charges are specific. If they charge assault, for instance, they must inform you of when, where, who, how, etc., or you have the right to ask for a "Bill of Particulars." If they charge that you were simply "inciting to riot," for instance, without alleging any facts, such as that you said thus and so under such and such circumstances, you cannot defend yourself because there is no telling what they will claim in court. They can claim almost anything. To guard against this, you have the right to a "Bill of Particulars" and should file the same sort of paper described above, but title it, "Motion for Bill of Particulars." Then write as follows: COMES NOW THE DEFENDANT IN THE ABOVE ENTITLED CAUSE, and moves the Honorable Court for a Bill of Particulars stating:

(Sample questions)

a. What specific acts are alleged to have been committed?

b. Who committed them?

c. What is the weapon the defendant is alleged to have used? (etc.)

Sign your name at the bottom and write "pro se" (for himself).

The special value of a Bill of Particulars is that once the Prosecutor has set down what he claims you did, he is strictly limited to proving those claims, and no others he can ring in on you! This is a tremendous help, especially with the phony, rigged-up charges they usually bring against nigger-fighters, etc. By their very rottenness, they tend to be loose, general, and imprecise. You can put them on the spot by demanding they pinpoint exactly what they are charging.

Be sure to include at the end of your legal papers a "CERTIFICATE OF SERVICE." This is a written paragraph that states that you have delivered a copy of the legal papers to the Prosecuting Attorney. The "Certificate of Service" should be worded as follows:

CERTIFICATE OF SERVICE

I certify that I have delivered "in person (or deposited in the U.S. Mail postage prepaid), a true copy of the foregoing Motion to the District Attorney at his office in the____Building, Arlington County, Va., this____day, of January, 1965.

____
JOHN DOE, Pro Se

When you have your legal papers neatly typed (double-spaced), deliver a copy to the Clerk of the Court. The copy you deliver to the Clerk of the Court goes to the Judge who is hearing the case.

Next, deliver a copy in person or by mail to the prosecuting attorney. The prosecuting attorney is called by different titles in different parts of the country. He may be known as the District Attorney, Corporation Counsel, Commonwealth Attorney, Etc.

If you are ever charged with "inciting to riot," as the Jews call it, when you try to tell people the simple facts of the Jew-communist conspiracy, be sure to go to the library and get a copy of *The Law and Public Safety*, by Judge Harvey Blackstone. We have found this book to be a mine of information on defending yourself against such charges.

You should be allowed plenty of time to prepare your case. If they try to rush you on a charge, even if it's only a misdemeanor, you should request a "Continuance" from the court when you are called before it and respectfully explain that you need time to prepare. Make that a matter of record. Courts dare not rush you, on the record, for you will surely win a reversal on appeal.

While you are preparing your case, I most strongly recommend that you also marshal your facts in the form of affidavits (sworn statements) from your witnesses, so that you will know what they are going to say on the stand, and they can't "rat out" on you without committing perjury.

You must also subpoena some witnesses who aren't your friends. If you have no lawyer, you have the absolute right, under the Constitution, to have the court order the witnesses you need into court. Go to the clerk of the court and respectfully ask for "subpoena forms." Fill them out, and return them to the clerk, who will have them served on your witnesses. If there are some documents you need, make a motion, as described above, to the court (the judge), respectfully ask for a "Subpoena Duces Tecum?"—which is a fancy way of saying an order to produce documents—or other things in court. Describe what you need for evidence and why you need it, and ask the court to issue the Subpoena Duces Tecum for these things. If the request is reasonable, they will have to grant it.

Make everything a matter of record. Without an accurate record, you can't fight an appeal.

In places like Philadelphia, where almost all the clerks are vile, vicious Jews, you will often have to throw your legal papers over the counter at them, as we have to do, when they refuse to even accept them. If they throw them back, then you must go see a judge, and again make it a matter of record that you insist on filing simple motions with the court. If they deny this fundamental right—no matter what else they do or you do—you will win on appeal in a hurry. Once they know you mean business and know what you are doing, they slow down on this "won't accept" garbage. If all else fails, insist on seeing the judge personally to complain.

If they have seized you illegally and/or invaded your home illegally without a warrant, etc., no matter what they find as "evidence," make a "Motion to Suppress the Evidence" on the grounds that the evidence was illegally obtained. They will have to give such illegal "evidence" back to you and forget it as evidence. If that's their whole case, then move to dismiss, and they will have to grant it.

When you are ready for trial, remember to do your best to make a good appearance—not flashy, but conservative and well-dressed. I advise all my people to carry an attaché case. It is the "badge" of the attorney. If you are neatly and conservatively dressed, act with assurance, and carry an attaché case, you will get the respect they give attorneys in court, as a matter of subconscious reaction by clerks, marshals, and even the judge. If you dress like a hood, they will, conversely, be ready to slip you a few months in the jug on general principles before they start, just from experience with other hoods dressed in that manner.

Your demeanor in court is hugely important. Be super-respectful to the judge—be he Jew, nigger, or ape. (And I have seen some where it's hard to be sure which.) You should also be gentle and firm about your rights. I have actually had to defy threats of contempt to get simple rights in especially vile, Jew courts. You will be safe if everything is on the record and you are sure of your rights. But if you fail to insist on them at trial, they will say on appeal that you "waived" your rights—that you didn't want them, believe it or not! So stick up for what you must, but be as respectful and mannerly as you can while doing it. Never respond to baiting by either the DA or the judge. I have actually had a judge call me names and do everything short of spitting on me to provoke me to "contempt," but I was able to hold out. If you get mad, you are a dead duck in a courtroom.

Now for the trial.

It will open with the selection of a jury if it is a felony or a serious misdemeanor.

If your charges permit a jury trial, never take a "bench" trial, by a judge without a jury, no matter how much some lawyer or policeman, etc., tells you the judge is a real "pal," etc., etc. I have seen too many of our boys who insisted on listening to this siren song in spite of my warnings, packed off to prison for no crime except believing this cheap talk. A jury is your only safe hope of justice, because even the most honest judge can be put under tremendous personal pressure. Even some of the most courageous judges quail before a whole community hating both them and their families! Except in exceptional circumstances, insist on all rights you may have to a jury trial.

Next, in selecting the jury, you have a certain number of jurors you can kick off for no special reason at all. Save these as long as you can. Before you get to these "challenges," you should respectfully ask to have Negroes and Jews excluded from the jury. There will be complete coverage of this in later lessons. Suffice, for the present, to point out that our kind of activities are strongly anti-Jewish and anti-nigger, and it would be as unjust to put niggers and Jews on our juries as to put relatives of the Plaintiff on the jury trying a "civil suit" for damages. Even if they rule against you on the "no-Jews-and-niggers," make it a matter of record that you asked, as grounds for an appeal if you are wrongfully convicted. If you have a lawyer, these gentlemen will usually be horrified by the judge and the whole action, since you jeopardize their whole practice for very little reward. Consequently, when the judge comes on with the usual, "I want no talk of niggers and Jews, etc., here," the lawyer falls on his face, bowing and mumbling, "Yes, sir!" But remember, he doesn't do the prison time— you do. So insist on excluding niggers and Jews.

Once the jury is selected, the prosecutor will make his opening statement, in which he will tell the court and/or the jury what he expects to prove. He is not allowed to argue and reason at this time, and if he does so, you should respectfully object. He just presents what he hopes he will prove—his "case," as it's called.

When he is finished with his opening statement, you make yours. You may not argue, either, or present any evidence—just what you believe you will show as your case.

You can sometimes, with the court's permission, reserve your "opening statement" until the time for you to put on your evidence. I recommend you ask for this permission when the prosecutor has finished presenting his opening statement. Ask the court for "Permission to Reserve my Opening Statement." If not granted, go ahead and state your case briefly and to the point. Never bore a court or look "lost." If you can't think of what to say next, say to the judge, "May I beg the court's indulgence for a few moments?" and, when it is granted, look at some papers, etc., until you recover your composure.

After you have either stated your case or reserved your opening statement, you should then get up and ask the court for "The Rule on Witnesses." This means that all witnesses on both sides will first be sworn, and then sent out of the court to wait in a witness room, where they cannot hear what other witnesses testify. This protects you, to some degree, from perjury and collusion. This motion has to be granted, and you should be sure all your witnesses come forward, are sworn, and sent into the jury room.

The prosecutor will then call his first witness and begin questioning him to present his evidence. He is severely restricted in his ability to ask his own witnesses questions. He may not ask questions that "lead" the witness. By and large, these are "yes" and "no" questions, in which he can put together a long string of claims and ask his witness if they are true—thus, in effect, testifying instead of the witness. If he asks leading questions, you must get up and object. If you do not do this at the time, you can't appeal later on these grounds!

There are several other kinds of questions he may not ask, and you should become very familiar with these types of questions. Here they are, briefly: (1) Questions requiring the witness to give an opinion or a conclusion, such as "Was the defendant drunk?" (the witness may testify that defendant was staggering, couldn't pronounce his words, and smelled, of alcohol, but it is for the jury to decide whether these facts indicated he was "drunk"); (2) Questions not directly related to the case at hand. If the defendant has not testified, for instance, a witness may not testify to the defendant's previous criminal record, nor may he testify, in a disorderly conduct case, for instance, that the defendant didn't love his wife, etc.; (3) immaterial questions—questions which would not affect the case, regardless of answer; and (4) incompetent questions—that is, questions which may not be asked. For instance, the prosecutor may not ask a man if the defendant did so and so—if the defendant is her husband, since spouses may not testify against each other. Nor could a doctor testify what his patient told him, etc.

If the prosecutor gets some answers from his witnesses he doesn't like, and starts to bully his own witness, you can object, since that is forbidden.

As the prosecutor finishes examining each witness, he will turn him over to you for cross-examination.

This will be the subject of an entire lesson, as it is the most important weapon patriots have against perjurers.

But I will state here that you should never cross-examine under the following conditions:

(1) When the evidence given didn't hurt you at all. If the witness merely testified that you possess a gun, and it is legal to possess a gun, there's no need to carry the matter further.

(2) When the evidence has almost smashed you, it is true, and you are sure you can't shake the witness. If you get up there and ask the same things the prosecutor did, it will reinforce all the horror of that damning testimony with the jury and hurt you far, far worse than saying "No questions."

(3) When the witness is obviously too much for you. (And this is not implying you are a slouch.) A weepy, old Jewish lady, for instance, who is sharp, will hurt badly, no matter what a vicious liar she may be. I have seen these Jewesses lie like hell, weeping piteously, as they describe how they were "persecuted," ad infinitum. The only way you could break them down and demonstrate what liars they are is to hammer at them unmercifully on details, but this would bring down upon you such concentrated wrath of court, jury, and spectators that it isn't worth it. The "concentration camp victim" they always trot out to snivel and weep in our trials is pretty deadly. The only exception is when they are foolish enough to bring on one who is really hysterical. With these, I have often been successful in drawing them out with more and more of their sob story—until, finally, they get so carried away that they tell such fantastic stories that it gets ridiculous! When there are snickers from the audience, these kikesses get raging wild and quit the sob-sister act and begin to act like old-fashioned Jews. But your chances of being able to get these results, I have found, are pretty slim. The Jews are too good as actors.

I will cover the whole subject of cross-examination in great detail in a future lesson. Until then, suffice it to say that the key to breaking liars is always detail. Try to get a liar to commit himself to more and more details about the story he has lied about, and sooner or later, he'll forget and swear to two mutually impossible "facts."

After you are finished with a witness, if your cross-examination has hurt him, the prosecutor will proceed with "re-direct" examination to repair the damage. If he does, you then have the right to "re-cross" examine the witness, and so on. Every time there is a direct, you have the right to cross.

When both sides are finished, the next witness is called, and so on until the prosecutor is finished presenting his witnesses. When he says "The prosecution rests its case," you should, as a matter of course, stand up and say "I move the court to dismiss the charges (or direct a verdict of acquittal) on the grounds that the prosecution has not presented a prima facie case, and we should not be required to come forward with a defense." This motion is based on the fact that the prosecution is required to present a solid case against you before you are required to defend yourself. If they have not, an honest court will throw the whole thing out, and you are free! We have won quite a few of such motions. But even if you don't win right there and then, you prepare excellent grounds for appeal later by this motion.

If the judge denies your motion (which is usual), then you should either come forward with your opening statement (if it was reserved, as suggested at the beginning) or call your first witness.

I recommend calling the weakest witnesses first and building up to the strongest, since most people's memory is unbelievably short and they tend to remember your last witnesses best.

Should YOU testify for yourself?

There are several vital factors involved in making that decision.

First, unless you are a "good witness," that is, unless you are sincere and able to make a judge and jury really feel that sincerity, "you will usually do little good testifying for yourself, especially with a judge only. They all know you want to get "loose" and figure you will say anything to do it. This discounts your testimony more than anybody else's, except co-defendants. And if you aren't too good at appearing in public, if you make a hesitant and weak witness, you will hurt yourself, no matter how innocent.

Second, if you testify, you forfeit your right not to have your past record brought up. If you take the stand, you give the DA the right to "impeach" your testimony by showing what a dirty "crook" you were, regardless of how much you have reformed or for how long, as have most of our fighting men. They can make you tell everything you ever did, all your arrests, convictions, prison terms, etc. Thus, if you have a "bad record," stay off the stand.

Third, if you get up there to testify as your own witness, you also forfeit your right to take the Fifth Amendment on questions involving guilt on other criminal acts; they may try to stick you with things long forgotten and past. Remember that you cannot invoke the Fifth Amendment if you voluntarily get up there on the witness stand. They cannot make you testify, nor even comment on the fact that you did not testify, to prejudice the jury. But once you get up there of your own accord, you are fair game and have no protection at all.

My own recommendation to my own men is, if in any doubt, don't testify. If you are sure of yourself and are on good, solid ground with a good record, you can help yourself. But the chances of helping are far less than the chance of catastrophe if you are not a "strong" witness or you have a record that can be made to look bad.

Now the tables are turned, and the prosecutor will object if you ask leading, irrelevant, or improper questions. Try not to do it, as sustained objections make you look bad and unfair to the jury.

The best questions to ask, I believe, are "Tell, in your own words, what, if anything, happened to you on (date) at 3 p. m.," etc. Do not ask questions that can be answered "Yes" or "No" in general.

You may want to "repair damage" after the DA cross-examines, and he will then re-cross, etc., as when he was putting on his witnesses.

You will often have documents that are vital to your case and that you will want to make part of the record of the case. This has to be done in a very precise, technical way.

First, take the document to the court's clerk sitting near the bench—usually the stenographer. Ask him or her to "please mark this document for identification." He or she will mark a number or letter on the document or item and say, into the record, that it is now marked "Exhibit ____ for identification." This does not mean it is in evidence, only that it is identified in the record. Then show the item to the prosecutor for his examination.

Now you must take the document or object to your witness who knows what it is and can testify, from personal knowledge, what it is. If it is a photo, for instance, it must be the photographer or a person completely familiar with the scene. Hand the witness the item and say, "I now hand you Exhibit________, for identification, and ask you if you know what it is?" When he answers "Yes," ask him to tell the court and jury what it is, and everything else you can ask him to make it abundantly clear that the item or document is definitely connected with the case and good evidence. When that has been thoroughly established, and not before, you may then ask the court to introduce it into evidence. If the court agrees, give it back to the clerk, who will mark it with a new number or letter as evidence.

When you rest your case, you will then have the right to make your "argument" or "close" to the court and/or the jury. If it is before a judge alone, stick to the law and the facts. You will not get the judge to snivel with tear-jerking stories, or his heart pitty-patting with your flag-waving, etc. In fact, it is my experience that the judge is usually writing his sentence while you are "closing." But if there is a jury, this is the time to come on with weeping, wailing, gnashing of teeth, the Constitution, motherhood, and anything else you feel will move the jury. After all, you want that jury to believe you and free you—and the best way to do that is to make them like you and love your cause. In our political trials, this is the only chance you'll have to reach the good, White Christians on that jury.

And remember, it takes only one of them to "hang" the jury, and if you reach the heart of that one juror, he will hold out forever, just as you are now fighting for what you believe, in spite of hell itself.

After you have closed, the judge will "charge" the jury—that is, he will tell them the law as it applies to the case. You have the right to insist that certain "instructions" be given to the jury. This is a very important, but also very technical matter, and cannot be covered here. I will simply suggest that you go to the nearest law library and get the book showing the possible "instructions" in your state for that particular case. Then insist on the ones that help you and you have a right to. You can also object to instructions proposed by the prosecutor.

When the jury has been charged, it will retire and reach a verdict. When they return and announce it—if it is "Not Guilty"—your troubles are over.

But if it is "Guilty," then you have the right to make a statement before sentencing. If the judge is obviously relishing the "hanging," don't bother, but if he seems decent at all, it may be worthwhile appealing to him and trying to make him see how wrong it is to let the Jews, niggers, and Communists push White Christian patriots around, etc.—and what is happening to our poor country and race.

As soon as the sentence is pronounced, you should immediately say, "Would Your Honor please set an appeal bond?" If you fail to do this, it is hard to get you out on bond later and takes a long time.

With that, they will probably drag you back to jail to await bail, and the struggle will be over, for a while.

Let me close this lesson on basic trial law with the stern reminder that whatever the jury decides are the facts, are decided forever. You can appeal the law and technicalities, but you cannot appeal the facts. Those are frozen forever at the trial, barring something wrong with the trial itself. It therefore behooves you to make a damned good job of the trial to see that the true facts are brought out in spite of liars and Jew "persecutors."

The best way to do this is to **work**. Work, study, and prepare as you have never done anything else in your life.

If you know your onions when you get up there in court, you will leave the Jew and nigger "persecutors" gasping for breath as we have often done.

Next Lesson: HOW TO DEAL WITH IMPROPER "INTERROGATION" METHODS, "third degree", bullying, entrapment, etc.

LESSON NO. 1

Test Questions

SELF-STUDY QUESTIONS

Type or print the Answers to these questions neatly on a separate sheet of paper, then send them in for correction and grading.

1. What is the most important principle of effective radical, racist, political operation?

2. Why is this principle so important?

3. You are stopped on the street while handing out literature by a detective. What is the first thing you should be sure of?

4. Why?

5. What must a policeman do before he has the right to force you to go with him?

6. What is the most important thing to know if you are falsely and wrongfully arrested by a police officer in uniform?

7. On the way to the police station in the patrol wagon you are punched without cause by a policeman. What should you do about it, and when?

8. What are your rights when you are "booked"?

9. What do you do if bail is set astronomically high?

10. What sort of attitude toward authorities should a political leader have while in custody?

11. You are charged with inciting to riot, penalty two years to ten years. Is this a misdemeanor or a felony?

12. You are charged with assault with a deadly weapon, penalty up to ten years. While in jail trying to raise bail, the Public Defender's Officer sends in a lawyer to help you. He tells you the District Attorney will let you "cop a plea" (plead guilty) to a lesser charge of simple assault, and that if you don't accept, you are. likely to do a long stretch in prison. What should you do?

13. What is the most important rule when charged with a felony?

14. Are there any times when you should appear in court in clothes other than a suit?

15. What proceeding are you entitled to after you are arrested and before you are tried on a serious charge?

16. What is the best protection against a bullying, vicious judge?

17. What is the first thing you should insist on at the hearing if you are facing a serious charge?

18. Why is it so important to dismiss a lawyer who is incompetent or selling you out?

19. Name the occasions when you should, plead "guilty" to serious charges.

20. Why? Explain.

21. What are the two basic sources when you are looking up the law?

22. Name a common defect of the political charges we usually face, and what should you do about it?

23. Without referring to the lessons, write up a complete motion to dismiss a charge of "disorderly conduct" against you, in the local police court of your area, in which it is alleged that you handed out anti-race-mixing literature where there was no law against such literature distribution.

24. Write up a motion for a Bill of Particulars for your own court, asking for details of charges against you that you "incited to riot."

25. What should you do if you are too rushed and cannot be ready for trial as scheduled?

26. How do you get reluctant witnesses into court to testify to important facts in your case?

27. How do you force the police or other parties to bring important documents or photographs, etc., that you need into court?

28. What should you ask in the selection of a jury? Why?

29. Make up a skeleton outline of the steps involved in a criminal trial.

30. When should you NOT cross-examine, and why?

31. What is the basic method of catching perjurers on

cross examination?

32. What should you do when the prosecution says, "Prosecution rests its case"?

33. When should you ask leading questions of your own witnesses?

34. What are the most common objections to questions on direct examination?"

35. How should you phrase most of your questions to your own witnesses?

36. If you have any doubt of what a witness will say on the stand, what is the best way to ensure that he won't switch his stories on you?

37. Give a step-by-step outline of what you must do to get a document, photograph, or object admitted into evidence in your case?

38. If the jury brings in a verdict of "guilty" against you, what motion should you make to the court on the spot?

39. What can you appeal about your case, and what can you NOT appeal from a jury verdict?

40. What is the one thing you must do, above all others, to ensure victory in your trial?

LESSON NO. 2

Dealing With Law Enforcement Agencies

It is impossible to lay down any hard-and-fast rules for dealing with police officers, FBI agents, other investigative and law-enforcement agencies, jailers, and prisoners. There are simply too many possible situations and personalities involved. However, a clear understanding of the working conditions, habits, and psychology of these groups is tremendously helpful in deciding what course of action to take in any given situation.

The first thing to realize when dealing with all these people is that it is almost impossible for them not to develop abnormal psychological reactions while engaged in their professional work.

Only on very, very rare occasions—sometimes never—does the average citizen encounter the possibility of being physically attacked by desperate and dangerous individuals. But the men and women engaged in the profession of law enforcement, investigation, and prison administration face this situation almost every day of their lives. Further, their life experiences are saturated with criminal contacts. Outside of the relatively few hours of their personal lives, they are continually dealing with subversive, criminal, and vicious human beings. This is particularly true of prison officials, jailers, and detectives.

The predictable and inevitable result on their personalities is that they become far more cynical and suspicious than the average person. Some of them tend to become somewhat brutalized by brutal experiences, and their natural defense mechanisms create an extremely authoritarian, tough, sometimes mean, and even occasionally brutal and sadistic personality.

It is an actual and amazing fact that both experienced criminals and (unfortunately) White, Christian patriots can usually spot detectives, FBI agents, etc., almost as easily as if they were wearing uniforms and badges. It is not only their black Chevys, Plymouths, and Fords, with the tiny antennas, their clean-cut hard look, their fedoras, and even sometimes trench coats, their almost universal appearance in pairs, or some of their "Dick Tracy" antics, which unmistakably stamp this breed as detectives and agents. Rather, it is a life of daily mastery over other human beings, whom they put in chains, handcuffs, and lockups, which stamps the faces of these men with an indefinable stern visage that instantly identifies these professional officers to both experienced criminals and patriotic fighters.

Perhaps a simpler way to express the above idea would be to say that professional law enforcement officers usually look the exact opposite of peace-creeps, weaklings, and liberals. Unlike most of our degenerate populace, these men must be in good physical condition, ready to fight physically and with weapons at any moment in defense of their lives and those whom they are paid to protect. They are men of force! The same granite look of stern authority and force may be seen in the visage of most of the men in early America, and pretty much for the same reason.

Precisely because they are men of force and physical combat, they tend to be diametrically opposed in personality to Jews, Communists, and the "ban-the-bomb" sissies, peace-creeps, cowards, and general scum now proliferating in all western "democracies."

I cannot emphasize the next point strongly enough. PRECISELY BECAUSE MOST LAW ENFORCEMENT OFFICERS ARE STRONG, MASCULINE, AND COURAGEOUS MEN, THEY INSTINCTIVELY DESPISE THE ENEMIES WE FIGHT—COMMUNIST JEWS, HELL RAISING NIGGERS, AND COWARDLY PEACE-CREEPS! AND, CONVERSELY, THEY INSTINCTIVELY ADMIRE COURAGEOUS AND OPEN FIGHTERS FOR OUR CAUSE.

In short, law enforcement officers and investigative agents are, by their very natures, our natural allies. To be sure, working for corrupt and Communist politicians, as they are forced to do, they are often obliged to deal harshly and even wrongfully with us. Most of them, the veterans, have long seniority in their careers and know no other profession or way of earning a living. Faced with direct orders to arrest or harass us, they have only the alternative of giving up their entire careers and retirement benefits, starving their families, and still accomplishing nothing, since other officers would take their place. It should never be forgotten that it was the staunch, White, Christian patriot, General Edwin A. Walker, who commanded the troops who stuck bayonets in the backs of teenage white girls in Little Rock. I never cease to be amazed—and disgusted—with the patriots who blast all law enforcement and investigative officers as "Communists" for following their orders from higher up. I never forget how these conclusion-jumpers insisted that the army at Little Rock and its commanders were "Communists." The same thoughtless patriots insist that all the U.S. marshals at Oxford, Mississippi, were also a bunch of "Jews," "Communists," etc. One of the top marshals at Oxford was one of our dedicated supporters! I cannot emphasize strongly enough to students that law enforcement officers, investigators, and jailers should be dealt with as PROFESSION-

ALS, not treated as vindictive and hateful enemies.

To be sure, FBI agents work for the Jew-ridden "Justice" Department, and the marshals and policemen often are forced, by orders from superiors and politicians, to act in a most hateful and seemingly vicious manner against us.

In most cases, their hearts are not only not in their work, but they find such assignments thoroughly distasteful and hateful. Given half a chance, they will do everything short of violating professional ethics to give us a break and make things as easy as possible.

However, IF YOU ACT LIKE A CRIMINAL HOODLUM AND A VICIOUS "COP-HATER" TOWARD THESE MEN, THEY WILL UNDERSTANDABLY DEVELOP A PERSONAL HATRED OF YOU AND WILL TREAT YOU ACCORDINGLY.

Now remember, as stated above, law officers, investigators, and jailers are especially conditioned to dealing with vicious and hateful characters. At the slightest sign of such characteristics in YOU, in spite of themselves, all their instincts drive them to act toward you as they do toward gangsters and deadly criminals.

If, on the other hand, you act in a responsible, quiet, dignified, and fearless professional manner, YOU DISARM THIS INSTINCTIVE REACTION. I have proved again and again with all of these kinds of officers, that it is possible to win their open admiration and at least covert friendship—providing you never permit yourself to be goaded into acting "wise," "tough," or in any way showing either fear or defiance.

Once, in New-Orleans Parish Prison, after a "line-up," a six-foot-four, 250-pound deputy sheriff took me away from the rest of my group and threw me in an isolated cell at the rear of the jail.

"Now, you no-good son-of-a-bitch," this monstrous brute growled as he gathered himself at the door of the cell to spring at me. "I'm going to find out just how tough you *!?**¢! sons-of-bitches are!"

The temptation to snarl and curse back at him was terrific. I wanted either to leap at him or try to squeeze out between the bars somehow.

But I did neither. Instead, with a supreme effort of will, I sat down on the steel bunk, folded my hands across a knee, and looked up at this towering brute as though he were coming to get my permission to do something.

"Do you have something else besides fists?" I asked him. "And are you man enough to tell me WHY you want to tear me up first?"

"Sure, I'll tell you, you *!©**!" he roared. "You Communist nigger-lovin' sons-of-bitches oughta be shot, every last God-damned one of you!"

"Nigger lover?!" I exploded. "I'm down here to do all I can, FIGHTING these Communist race-mixing 'freedom riders'!"

"Didn't you come down here on one of them 'freedom rides'?" he asked, slowing down a bit.

"Hell, no!" I replied. "I hate those Red bastards worse than you do!"

The big deputy relaxed a little more, and some of the redness went out of his face and neck.

"But ain't you one of them Nazis?"

"Yes, sir, I am the leader of the Nazis," I answered. "But if you will remember, Hitler believed the Whites are a 'master race' and so do I. We are almost all U.S. combat veterans and believe in a White, Christian America—and we're ready to fight. We're sick of niggers, Communists, and Jew traitors! In fact, I am leading a 'hate bus' down here to oppose ...."

The deputy stepped back and leaned against the bars. "I thought you people were a bunch of Germans and Communists," he said quietly. "I've been reading ...."

He finally sat down on the bunk beside me and, after more than an hour of earnest conversation, wound up with the conclusion that the only thing wrong with us was our name (as usual).

Can you imagine what would have happened to me had I reacted instinctively by snarling and swinging? That is what has happened to thousands and thousands of people who act on feelings and fear rather than on reflection and consideration.

By no means am I saying that you will be able to avoid all persecution and beatings by professionalism and forbearance.

There will be occasions, particularly when you are confronted with Jew jailers or cops and detectives, when the only thing you can do is defend yourself and your life if necessary.

On the other hand, Jews tend to be bullies, and bullies are overbearing and brutal when they have the upper hand but swinish and cringing when the situation is reversed. Ordinarily, I recommend not resisting officers even under extreme provocation, but when you are being unmercifully beaten and may face serious injury or death at the hands of some Jew terrorist wearing a policeman's uniform, once you decide to resist, I recommend MAXIMUM and as brutal a resistance as possible.

On the other hand, when dealing with a single Negro, I have often found that they are so child-like in their reactions, and can change so quickly from anger and brutality to thigh-slapping laughter and cackling, that if you can manage to get them laughing, you can be pretty sure of avoiding any serious beating.

A group of Negroes is something else again. When there are more than two of them, they have a powerful gang instinct, which is particularly murderous, and any attempts at humor are wasted. Mobs and gangs, however, are, like bullies, notoriously cowardly. When faced with a beating by such a gang, your only hope is to convince them that, while they would probably overpower you, any one of them would also probably wind up beaten and gouged and perhaps with broken bones at the very least.

Most of the inmates of most prisons are Negroes, and even in the South, they are being mixed more and more. In jail, you will be faced with many situations where niggers use terrorism for extortion, brow-beating, and pleasure. My recommendation when faced with such a situation, when first thrown into such an institution where niggers are allowed to terrorize the White prisoners, is to pick one of the toughest who tries to mistreat you and go at him hammer and tongs with all you've got, even though it means a sure trip to the "hole." You will probably get torn up some and will certainly spend time in the hole, but most of the terrorists and bullies will leave you severely alone when you are known as one who will fight at the drop of a hat.

WHATEVER YOU DO IN PRISON, NEVER BECOME A "BUDDY" WITH THE GUARDS. IT COULD COST YOU YOUR LIFE! Speak to them only when necessary and then with no more courtesy than absolutely necessary. This is a crazy situation—there can be no doubt of that, but it is simply a factual situation with which you must deal realistically. "Finks" and "stoolies" and even just "pals" of the guards may win some temporary advantages, but these will be far outweighed by the deadly danger such characters face from close contact 24 hours a day, 7 days a week, with desperate and dangerous men.

If you are a young man and good-looking, you will inevitably be faced with the vile homosexual creatures who will want to make a "punk" or a "queen" out of you. This unspeakable horror goes on all the time in almost all prisons and jails, and is one of the reasons why I believe in working to eliminate prisons and jails and returning to corporal punishment.

If you are the young type who is attractive to these filthy degenerates, beware of "favors" from older convicts. They will start offering you all sorts of "extras" in the hope of winning your cooperation for their filthy purposes.

Usually, if you refuse to succumb to such blandishments, one or more of them will gang up to "rape" you. I have seen this unspeakable atrocity happen in spite of all a poor kid could do. This is one of the foul and filthy marks against our supposedly civilized and advanced society. I can only advise that if you ever face this ultimate horror, fight as you never have before. Death, in my opinion, is a minor matter compared to the living death of kids who are thus seduced or "raped" and themselves turned into repulsive prison homosexuals.

If you know you must go to prison as you very well may, while waiting appeals you know you will lose, you should learn typing, bookkeeping, and library work. Typists are urgently needed in prisons, and you will find out that your treatment will be vastly different if you have something they need in the prison. They need typists and clerical help. If you can supply this need, your life will be at least 25 and maybe 50% better than if you are forced to join the rock-busting gang.

THE THIRD DEGREE

With the sophistication of police methods in the last 30 or 40 years, and a series of Supreme Court decisions assiduously protecting the "rights" of criminals, with little regard for the rights of society, you will rarely find yourself subjected to the old-fashioned "third degree" methods of interrogation. To be sure, you will often be interrogated for long periods without rest or comfort and perhaps even under blaring lights, etc., but you will rarely be beaten or otherwise physically mistreated, unless you make the fatal mistake, covered in the last lesson, of acting "wise" and "hoody."

Nevertheless, you will most certainly run into some devilish efforts to incriminate you—sometimes illegally and falsely.

I have already covered one of the most prevalent of such methods of interrogation in the previous lesson—the "Good Guy—Bad Guy Technique."

Much more prevalent, however, is the simple and ancient method of interminable questions.

We have already pointed out, as strongly as possible, that WHEN CHARGED WITH A FELONY OR A SERIOUS OFFENSE OF ANY SORT, YOU SHOULD NEVER GIVE MORE THAN YOUR NAME AND ADDRESS. But in this lesson on methods of interrogation, etc., I want to expand and emphasize this all-important point.

In order to be able to resist clever interrogation, you must thoroughly understand the PSYCHOLOGY that you will face.

Students who have not already done so are strongly urged to read and study the book *The Battle For the Mind* by William Sargant. (Penguin Books, Inc., 1961). This book will give you a clear understanding of the fact that the most deadly danger in facing those who attempt to wheedle or force you to say or admit something against your will is that you will become EMOTIONALLY INVOLVED. Conversely, your greatest safeguard against slick or bullying interrogators is complete emotional detachment.

As advised in a previous lesson, you should never, never, never even open your mouth to interrogators when charged with a serious crime. You should not listen to offers, inducements, threats, "tips," or any other brandishments designed to get you to talk against your will.

But you should go further.

In order to discourage tough and persistent interrogators, who would otherwise exhaust you and press you unmercifully, you should defeat them psychologically at the very outset by giving such an appearance of absolute, stony, and utterly unbreakable SILENCE that they quickly realize that further efforts of any kind will be completely useless and perhaps even make fools of them.

In the face of particularly rough and bullying interrogators, I recommend going so far as to actually close your eyes and refuse to open them—or your mouth.

Retreat completely within yourself and build such a wall of stony silence around you that your would-be inquisitors cannot help getting the feeling they are raging at a dead man.

In using this technique, remember that they will make every effort to shock, surprise, and scare you into a reaction—ANY reaction. And the slightest such reaction on your part, no matter what they say or do, destroys all the effect of the silence you have maintained, perhaps for hours. So, once you have determined not to talk, which is your absolute right, stick with it to the death.

One of the favorite tricks of interrogators is to use phony "evidence" that your companions and associates have "already told us everything." Therefore, it goes without saying, believe absolutely nothing you are told or shown or "happen" to see, which promotes this idea. The thought that you alone are left holding the bag, and will get maximum punishment, while your associates are all busily squealing and cooperating with the police to railroad you to the penitentiary, is the single most frequent cause of "breaking" in those who know that they should not talk. And once they have been able to get YOU to talk, they use your statement to break the others the same way.

So I repeat, and cannot repeat often enough, if charged with a serious crime, and/or felony. DO NOT TALK!

ENTRAPMENT

It is everywhere illegal for-police officers or anybody else to PROCURE the commission of a crime, which would otherwise not have happened.

There is much misunderstanding of this doctrine. Just because a police agent is working with you when you commit an illegal act, you are not thereby excused from responsibility and punishment.

To constitute entrapment, the police officer or agent must be directly responsible for GETTING you to commit the illegal act, and it must be shown by you that, had it not been for the police officer or agent, YOU WOULD NOT HAVE COMMITTED THE ACT.

Thus, if a group of men got together and conspired to throw stink bombs into a Communist race-mixing meeting in a nigger church, and a police agent was merely present at such a gathering, but did not suggest the stink-bombing, there would be no entrapment, and all those present could be convicted of the conspiracy and the act.

On the other hand, if the police agent actually suggested the stink-bombing, it was opposed by the membership, and it was only because of the pressure and influence of the police agent that the act took place, the police agent is guilty of "entrapment," and the other participants cannot be convicted.

Experience has shown, in cases all over the country, that the Jews go after our kind of people everywhere by using, not policemen, but agents of the Anti-Defamation League or other Jewish groups to do the actual promotion of the illegal and violent acts, while a policeman or other law enforcement agent is merely present.

I will not here go into the philosophy of violence versus legal methods of winning power. Suffice to say that I believe the Civil War and the constant beating down of the Ku Klux Klan have convinced me that we can be SUCCESSFUL only by legal and elective methods.

And to succeed by such methods, we must stay out of Jew dungeons. And to stay out of Jew dungeons, we must survive the constant efforts of Jewish agents to provoke and ensnare us into impatient acts of senseless violence which do not hurt the enemy (and in fact give him "martyrs"), while they salt some of our best men away in penitentiaries.

Therefore, one of the most important lessons in this course is to rid yourself once and for all of the last vestiges of the old-fashioned "criminal code" or false "loyalty" which decrees that you must never "squeal" on those who advocate and promote violence and illegal acts.

Ever since "L.E. Rogers," the enemy agent, tried to promote synagogue bombing in our Atlanta group, after which the Jews blew up their own synagogue and then tried to electrocute our brave young men on the testimony of Jew-stooge Rogers, I have watched dozens of fine young patriots dumped into Jew dungeons because they did not know how to deal ruthlessly with Jewish agents provocateurs in their ranks.

When you hear someone counseling and promoting dangerous and illegal acts of violence, which could send all of your group to the penitentiary, YOU MUST PRESUME HE IS AN ENEMY AGENT!

I realize that there are some among us who have concluded that we cannot win by peaceful methods and counsel such acts. I sympathize with the good instincts of these men, but deplore their defeatism and foolishness, tactically speaking. They play directly into the hands of our most deadly enemies. I wish them no harm and would protect them as much as possible from the results of their own foolishness.

But the fate of White, Western, Christian civilization and of our fighting organizations depend on our ability to remain out of prison and keep fighting. More dangerous than beatings, assassination attempts, or any other threat to us, is the agent provocateur who gets us discussing and scheming acts of illegal violence in the presence of police agents.

Therefore, I cannot over-emphasize the absolute necessity for dealing with all those who advocate violence and illegal acts as enemy agents. When a visitor comes to me and starts talking bombs, dynamite, beatings, and killings, I instantly stop him and warn him that further such talk must be taken seriously, and I will be forced to turn him in to the authorities. There are short-sighted patriots, I am aware, who will indignantly snort that I am a fink and rat, etc., for even mentioning "turning in" possible patriots. But let me point out to all students that, if the promoter of violence and criminal acts is NOT a patriot, but an agent or provocateur, and you fail to report his conspiracy, and a criminal act then occurs, you are well on your way to prison.

As a case in point, I might mention young Don Branch of Miami who got carried away with the "pitch" of the "Minutemen," and wound up in a car with a Jew agent and a bundle of sawed-off broom sticks supposed to be dynamite, who is NOW DOING 20 YEARS IN THE FLORIDA PENITENTIARY for being "loyal" and "decent"' to one of these filthy agents.

On the other hand, one cannot frivolously serve up as human sacrifices every foolish and hot-headed patriot who may "talk bad."

What I recommend, in such cases, is that you immediately warn those who insist on "talking bad" that you will not hear any more such talk, and that if the visitor or friend continues in the same manner, you will be forced to conclude he is an enemy agent and you will have no choice but to report him to the police or FBI.

If he persists in promoting such talk and activities among your group and in your presence, THEN YOU MUST INDEED TAKE STERN ACTION, heave him out and report his proposals to the proper authorities.

I repeat, this is not "squealing"; this is self-preservation!

The majority of all of our kind of people in jail are there because they did not protect themselves from this sort of enemy frame-up.

Do not go out of your way, of course, to learn details of the operation of those who may believe in fighting Communist treason by force and violence. You have no duty to do any such thing, nor to report what is none of your business.

But those who insist on forcing guilty knowledge of illegal activity on YOU AND YOUR ORGANIZATION are going out of their way to endanger you against your judgment and will. You cannot be soft and "loyal" to such foolish people, because too many of them are not friends, but outright enemy agents.

Therefore, I repeat, when visitors or new recruits "talk bad," stop them instantly and sternly, and warn them that any further such talk will be turned over to the authorities.

If they persist even after such a stern warning, you have no choice but to protect the organization and yourself from possible enemy action by turning these agents or damned fools in.

In the ranks of the Party, this is not advice; it is direct orders of the highest priority.

WOMEN AND LIQUOR

Our kind of people, Nazis, are, by nature, masculine, virile, and tend to be quite extreme in these characteristics.

This makes our kind of people especially vulnerable to two threats that have ever been dangerous to "he-men" from antiquity—liquor and women.

For this reason, neither I nor any of my officers touch a drop of any sort of alcoholic beverage. We simply cannot afford the luxury of "nirvana" or any partial loss of our faculties when we face all sorts of deadly danger 24 hours a day and seven days a week. I strongly recommend that students who contemplate a career of counter-revolutionary patriotism in defense of our White, Christian, Constitutional Republic against Jew-Communist treason and race-mixing, "take the oath" against alcohol as has all of our officer corps. In any case, if you must drink, never do it in public or where you have the slightest chance of meeting strangers or hostile individuals. In addition, if you MUST drink, try to be sure that one member of the group, at least, stays stone sober so that he can stop any dangerous "whisky talk" that may get started under dangerous circumstances.

On the other hand, while I preach asceticism for our hard-core counter-revolutionaries, it is my belief that no real male FIGHTER can successfully and healthfully live forever without the complementary benefits of the female designed by the Lord for all Nature. However, since beautiful women have been the classic weapon for reaching and destroying even the strongest and toughest leaders all through history, our fighters must learn steely self-control in dealing with their passions and the women who inevitably flock around courageous, fighting young men.

Over in Maryland, a group of young Jewish teenage girls actually succeeded in getting two of my young men convicted of statutory rape, by the oldest stratagems in the world. No amount of warning was successful in preventing this foreseeable foolishness, and I do not expect we will be able to eliminate it in the future.

But I cannot warn the student strongly enough against falling victim to his own rationalizations where a wench is concerned. Even good women, not working for the enemy and with the best of motives, have again and again proved the downfall of young men determined to fight for their race and nation in this greatest of all political battles.

I have no doubt that Mrs. Paul Revere was clinging to the neck of Mr. Revere on the night of 18 April 1775 and pleading, "Yes, Paul, but why you? Why can't some of the other men ride through Massachusetts to warn that the British are coming?"

I have seen some of our greatest fighting patriots, particularly generals and admirals, men who would face blazing hell itself, on wheels, scamper like rabbits in their own homes at the scratchy voice of their "Mrs."!

Thus, where chance "romances" are concerned, I staunchly recommend that our lads take the most extreme precautions against female agents, and CERTAINLY never listen to "sweet talk" from Jewish girls. Married fighters should face up to the fact that it is quite impossible to give one's maximum and total loyalty to both a wife and a counter-revolution. One or the other must play second fiddle. And it is not in the nature of either of these things to be content with the No. 2 spot. The student should therefore sit down quietly and calmly and reason out precisely what his major goal is in this life. If that goal is to be a 100% successful and superior husband and father, then he will have to be content with the Birch Society and the Boy Scouts. He will simply find it impossible to fight, as our grandpappies did in the revolution and all of their wars and battles, and also be a first-class husband and father in the so-called "modern tradition," where the husband and father is a sort of wage-slave and general handyman.

And if the student is determined to dedicate his life to an all-out FIGHT for ideals and for his race and Christian civilization, then he must teach his wife and family the same spirit of idealism and self-sacrifice—or he will inevitably lose them.

MINOR INTERROGATIONS

If relatively friendly detectives or FBI agents come to talk with you, and no serious charges are involved. I recommend that you do your best to be open and friendly with them and use the occasion to win not only their liking and respect, but their understanding of what we are trying to do.

I repeat, if serious charges are involved, or may be involved, you should say absolutely nothing. But if officers or FBI agents come to ask you about a literature distribution and that sort of thing, I heartily recommend that you cooperate to the limit and use the occasion to "de-brainwash" them—if they need it.

In doing this, I have found that the most effective possible weapon is HUMOR.

The officers usually try to be super dignified and reserved. Almost invariably, policemen, especially local police, will call you by your first name to give you the feeling that you are inferior and either a nigger or a little kid while they are in command of the situation. I recommend that you go along with this little game and be most respectful to them, even though they try to treat you like an irresponsible squirt. Sooner or later, your forbearance and dignity and success, coupled with their own silly little game (which is effective and a good thing with criminals), will make them feel inferior, instead of you.

Inevitably, they will confront you with a sort of machine-like procedure and formality behind which they hide their personal feelings.

You can disarm and "melt" this icy approach with gentle stabs of good humor that reach them. As an example, whenever I talk about Martin Luther King to detectives in a strange city and refer to him as "Martin Luther Coon," in spite of themselves, the detectives wind up chuckling. Then, if you can successfully follow this up while they are still smiling with a report of the latest doings of the "spooks" in your local area, etc., or an especially juicy "hatelet" from the *Stormtrooper*, etc., you will get them laughing over the niggers and Jews and establish a spirit of camaraderie which is hard for them to beat.

An even better example is the way I have been able to break through the icy reserve of almost all FBI agents by kidding them about their recent fink, Jake Levine.

Levine is a Jew who managed to sneak into the FBI, only to resign after gathering all the information he could, and joining up with all the leftist, pro-Communist, and Jewish outfits he could find ("surprisingly" enough!). On a New York radio station, he was interviewed and claimed that the FBI was fascist, anti-Semitic, and anti-Negro!

To all new FBI agents, I point out that their only fink in many years turns out, strangely enough, to have been a Jew, just like the Rosenbergs, etc., etc. They are understandably intensely proud of their esprit de corps and their loyalty to each other, etc., and when you point out that the only guy to "break the chain" was a nice Jew boy, you will often get a reaction which shows just how much the FBI loves Jews.

I never waste time telling them how many spies and traitors so many Jews are. They already know. And when you try to give them straight facts on the Jewish conspiracy, they are ready for you and rebuff you with their cold, professional manner.

But when you get them laughing, in spite of themselves, at the ridiculous Jews and niggers who have us all in an uproar, you have smashed through the glacier-like barrier of professional ice and reached their hearts.

In case you think this is rationalization or exaggeration, reflect that you would never get a professional Jew or nigger laughing at such matters. Rather, especially the Jews would be half out of their minds with hysterical hate, such as we have so often witnessed.

To sum up the essence of the art of dealing with police officials and investigative agents, you will have the battle 9/10ths won when you UNDERSTAND the psychology of these people and know how to put that understanding of their emotional workings to use.

If they are vile Jews, play on the fact that they are emotional and hysterical and cannot control themselves. Gently "stab" them with biting facts, truths, and your own attitude of utter superiority, which will have them climbing up the walls and screaming in helpless rage if you do it right. With niggers, try to get them laughing if possible and point out the way they are being used by Jews.

With police officers and agents who are neither Jewish nor Negro, if they are professional, meet them on their own grounds and be professional yourself. If faced with a minor matter, win their respect and liking by your conduct and get them laughing at the Jews and niggers in spite of themselves.

If faced with a serious charge—a felony—say nothing and DO NOT REACT. Sit back, close your eyes, close your mind, close your ears, close your mouth, and withdraw completely from the present situation.

In jail, let bullies and queers know in no uncertain terms and physically that any attempt to "mess" with you will mean losing a few teeth and a probable trip to the hole.

In dealing with those who approach you or your group with suggestions of violence and illegal activity, first warn the person that you will not tolerate any further such talk or suggestions, and that if he continues, you will be forced to conclude he is an agent provocateur and turn him in. If he thereupon continues to jeopardize you and your organization, TURN HIM IN.

In dealing with bullying jailers, never show either fear or the "wise guy" arrogance of the criminal hood.

Finally, and perhaps the most important single thing to remember from this whole lesson, if you are accused of a serious crime or felony, DON'T TALK!

LESSON NO. 2
Test Questions

SELF-STUDY QUESTIONS

1. Most law enforcement officers have developed ______ ____________ ________________ toward the people they deal with every day.

2. Policemen and policewomen face _____________ almost every day.

3. A policeman is more ____________ than the average person.

4. A policeman is the opposite of a ________________.

5. A policeman is a ________________ man.

6. Because of this, a policeman instinctively ______ our enemies, the Jews, niggers and peace-creeps.

7. Therefore, policemen, by their natures, are our _____ ________________.

8. Policemen often mistreat us because they don't want to lose their _______________.

9. However, if you act like a ______________, they will treat you like one.

10. In order to __________ them, act in a ________ manner.

11. Never act like a __________________ .

12. The Commander whipped the 250-pound jailer with ______________.

13. Under extreme provocation, you should_____ _____.

14. If you decide to resist, use _________ ___________.

15. A single Negro may be disarmed with ___________.

16. A gang of Negroes must be________ that at least one of them is going to be________________.

17. Explain what to do when confronted by mistreatment by prisoners.

18. What should you never do in prison?

19. _____________ are the most despicable creatures in a prison.

20. If you are approached by one, you should ________ .

21. ________ and ________ are needed skills in prison.

22. ___________ methods of interrogation are obsolete.

23. The most prevalent form of interrogation is the ____________ __________ technique.

24. When charged with a felony, or serious offense of any sort, you should give your _________ and _________ only.

25. A good book to read on brainwashing is__________ by ________________.

26. The interrogators are trying first and foremost to get you ___________ _________________.

27. To defeat them at this game, you should be ________.

28. When the interrogator says all your friends have "squealed" on you, you should tell them _______________.

29. If a police officer______you to commit a crime, this is ___________.

30. If a policeman is ________ but does not suggest the crime, it is not _________________.

31. Usually the ___________ promote illegal acts, while ________ are present, in order to convict the patriots.

32. The Civil War and Ku Klux Klan activities prove ___ methods are most successful.

33. You should _______ be loyal to those who promote violent and illegal acts.

34. When you hear someone promoting illegal activities, you must presume he is an _______ ____________.

35. When someone talks bad, you should ____ him that you will ______________________________.

36. This is not ____________; it is _______________.

37. Why should a Nazi be careful of his drinking habits?

38. It is impossible to give full loyalty to both a _____ and a ____________________.

39. The best weapon to use when talking to FBI men (when no serious charges are involved) is _____________.

40. All FBI agents are like Jake Levine. (True or false)

41. The key to 9/10 of the problem of dealing with policemen is ____.

42. If accused of a serious crime, ________ _________.

43. Summarize in your own words what your attitude should be toward:

(a) Policemen in general

(b) Policemen who have accused you of a-felony

(c) Men who suggest violent and illegal activity

(d) Fellow prisoners (all types)

(e) Prison guards

LESSON NO. 3
Surveillance & Countersurveillance

"BUGGING," SURVEILLANCE, AND COUNTER-SURVEILLANCE:

Before going into details on the subjects of "bugs," surveillance, etc., I must make two statements that may seem contradictory but will resolve themselves during the lesson.

The first statement is that the vast majority of right-wingers are almost paranoiac in their fear of surveillance, "spies," etc. To be sure, the Jews and their tools can be damnably mean and vicious in their frames and in the way some of them use police and detectives to harass us.

But I have, over the past decade, seen an almost endless parade of right-wing patriots who get so carried away with themselves and the air of conspiracy that you would think each one of them was Adolf Hitler personally, with the whole Israeli terrorist organization, the FBI, and everybody else after him PERSONALLY!

Once, when I was sitting in the front room of my Arlington headquarters with some visitors, a car raced by, shooting through the window. One of the visitors (a man I am sure not one American in a million has ever heard of) fell to the floor screaming, "They're after me, I told you! They hate me! They hate me worse than Hitler! Etc., etc." Admittedly, this is an extreme case. But I have met literally hundreds and hundreds of patriots who carry the "they're after-me" bit to foolish extremes.

Especially in the south, when I have visited some patriots, they go dashing about in automobiles as if they were starring in a Grade B spy movie, careening around corners, racing up alleys, etc., etc.,—when it is quite obvious nobody gives a damn where they are or what they're doing. The reason for much of this is that such carryings-on give these peanut-patriots a tremendous feeling of importance when they actually are unable to accomplish any real progress. In addition, a lot of them get a big kick out of dashing around, carrying huge pistols, and playing at "cops and robbers."

I cannot strongly enough advise responsible and intelligent fighters for our cause against this childish play-acting!

On the other hand, I must also say what will at first sound contradictory.

While I do not conduct myself in the childish manner of a Grade B spy movie hero, I DO presume that almost every word I say and every act I do is recorded on film, taped, etc., and I may someday sit and view the results in court.

As will be shown later, modern surveillance techniques and electronic equipment are such that there is almost no place on the face of this earth, nor below it, nor in the waters upon it, nor in the heavens above, that you can escape surveillance if professional and skilled experts are determined to keep you under surveillance.

Let me give just a few examples to show the Grade-B-movie-type right-wing "heroes" how foolish most of their gyrations and attempted "outwitting" of surveillants are.

Most people believe that, to be overheard in a room, it is necessary for the room to be "bugged." That has ceased to be true for more than 15 years.

Whenever you speak or make any noise whatsoever, you make invisible sound waves which actually move everything in the room about you, even though imperceptibly. Your voice—even a whisper—causes windowpanes in the room to oscillate like the diaphragm in a simple microphone or earphone.

Modern surveillance experts can take up station in a building that is blocks away from you, even across a river, etc., and bounce a beam of invisible light off your window, without ever bugging the room. As you move the window with your voice, it will "modulate" the light beam, and the resulting bounced return beam can be easily read by electronic devices at another station to hear every word you say.

Further, latest electronic developments have produced recording sets unbelievably tiny and actuated by the voice, so that they can sit waiting for weeks until you enter an area, and then they will broadcast every word you say. To bug a car, they do not have to do a lot of wiring. They have only to attach a small box no larger than a cigarette pack, which can be held by magnets under the dashboard, to pick up most of what you say and broadcast it to recorders.

To "tail" an automobile, professional agents no longer need to chase you around corners as in a gangster movie (although this is still done). They can walk by your car and attach a radio beeper even smaller than a cigarette case, which adheres by magnetism, anywhere to the underside of your car. This beeper will then pinpoint your location anywhere within a city to agents taking "cross bearings."

Tiny television pickups can be installed through holes not much bigger than a pin prick, so that you can be filmed and observed almost anywhere, regardless of your efforts at privacy.

I could go on and on and on. But my point is simply that those who go through a lot of rigmarole supposedly avoiding surveillance and recording are largely wasting their time with the old-fashioned "cops and robbers" methods they use.

There ARE very few ways to absolutely outwit surveillance, and they will be given below.

My point is that students of this course should make up their minds right now to quit playing any further games with detectives racing around in cars, etc.

In most cases, when you KNOW you are being followed, they WANT you to know.

Unless the agents are extremely clumsy (and I will admit some city detectives ARE clumsy), you will never know when they are REALLY keeping you under surveillance.

In many cases, particularly in the south, where many patriots still believe in the old Civil War and Klan methods of terrorism, both the FBI and detectives use what is called a "rough shadow"—obvious tailing—to harass suspected bombers, etc., and prevent them from committing illegal acts.

In spite of the fact that most of these people have the purest and holiest motives, and a good deal of most commendable courage, they fail to realize that, especially their bombing of "churches," even though these so-called churches are actually nigger revolution headquarters, do not help our cause. Every church bombing, such as the Birmingham church bombing, sets us back years because of the propaganda the press and the Jews can make of it as an "atrocity." Nor does it really stop the enemy by scaring them to death. It merely goads them to still further fanatical attack on the White Race and Western Christian civilization.

As I have pointed out many, many times in other writings, terrorism is not only never successful when partial; it is downright suicidal because it reinforces the enemy's will to resist and serves its propaganda cause. Therefore, as I have again and again counseled in this course (and in every other thing I have written or spoken), I adjure students and fighters for our cause to STAY LEGAL.

DON'T BREAK THE LAW! YOU DON'T HAVE TO!

As I have stated above, I presume that every word and every act of mine is filmed and recorded, and I may one day have to sit reviewing them in some courtroom, as has happened to the Communists many times. But by staying scrupulously legal, this not only does not hurt, it often helps.

It is quite impossible for them to frame me for a synagogue bombing, for instance, when I am under FBI surveillance.

I strongly suggest to all students that they conduct themselves so that they can sit back and enjoy the "show" any time they are confronted with films or tapes of their doings or conversations, in court or anywhere else.

Now, to get down to cases, even though you remain 100% legal, as we do, there are still times when it is imperative to make political plans that are safe from compromise and surveillance. We have such cases all the time in planning political demonstrations, which are legal but which require an element of surprise. For these purposes, I can pass along the secret of the ONLY way you can be relatively safe from surveillance.

When you wish to confer with an associate in absolute privacy, I recommend, as the only possible way to do it, that you go out into an open, outdoor area, always a different place and far from any dwelling or even bushes, if possible, and take along a transistor radio.

Then you should talk directly into the ear of your associate in as quiet a whisper as possible, while turning the transistor radio full on. The latter precaution is necessary because of the parabolic "shotgun" mikes available to surveillants. These latter devices have been so effective that they can be aimed like a gun across hundreds of yards and pick up whispers.

With the technique described, the radio will completely blackout your whispers, and unless your associate is a spy, you are quite safe from surveillance.

When necessary to discuss confidential matters in an automobile, you should use the same technique of speaking in your associate's ear and turn the radio on full blast.

In an emergency, you can use the same technique in a room, again turning a radio up full blast, although your security is far less.

ROUGH SHADOW

If, for any reason, you are ever subjected to an unfair and illegal "rough shadow," here is how you can get rid of it.

Do not race around town and into alleys and up and down highways a la spy movies. This is just what they want and is usually a waste of time. It is also dangerous.

If you are on foot and being tailed by a pack of detectives, as has often happened to me in some southern cities, response Number One is a camera. You should carry a small camera, preferably a miniature one, if possible. We have a Minox.

Walk briskly around a corner, stop, and turn around, aim the camera directly at the corner where the detectives should soon appear. As soon as they do, take their picture, look triumphant, and walk on. They will usually be nonplused for a while and quite surprised at this tactic, to say nothing of a little worried about what you might do with the photograph.

Tactic Number Two is to take a hotel or motel room, and start making cryptic, odd calls to all the pinko, disloyal race-mixing Unitarian ministers, peace-creeps, Commies, Zionists, and other scum in town, carefully keeping notes on a little pad of their names and addresses and telephone numbers.

When you have finished this, tear the memorandum notes into tiny pieces. Burn a few of them and throw the rest into the toilet. If the harassers have been particularly vicious, you can filthy up the scraps in the toilet a bit, too.

Then you can dash around to the back doors of some of the houses on the list. As the detectives come in sight, you should be coming back out of the back door, apparently stuffing papers or money in your pocket.

There are many more things you can do to harass the harassers, such as going to stations and asking for schedules of trains, planes, and buses to various destinations, etc., but these should suggest themselves to any thoughtful student.

When you are faced with an automobile-chase scene, I have found one of the most effective replies is to get the harassers careening around following you desperately, and then lead them all up a dead end, jump out of your car, and rush back to the leader of the pack, before he can get turned around, and ask pleasantly if you can be of any help to them.

Sometimes the officers, who are often disgusted with their assignment to harass you for the benefit of Jews and nigger-lovers, will break down right then and there and get decent and friendly, and you can put an end to the whole farce. If not, you can be sure they will be taken aback by such audacity and put into something of a panic trying to get back out of the cul-de-sac into which you have led them. They will all have very red faces. I have often done this.

After you have had all the fun you want with such foolish and illegal harassers, and you want to lose them, here is how to do it: Arrange to have someone of approximately your build and wearing the same type of clothes you have on in the men's room of a road house, service station or something of that sort on the main highway, where there is also a back entrance or window from the men's room.

After racing around a while, rush into the selected restaurant or service station, dash into the men's room, stand on one of the toilet seats, and crouch down, while your confederate runs out the back way, jumps in your car, and tears off down the road.

This technique is especially effective if you take the precaution, in advance, to wear very distinctive clothes, "hate" glasses, etc.—especially if you make an obvious attempt at "disguise"—which your confederate then duplicates.

If you are faced with a continuing, vicious, unfair, and political "rough shadow" over a period of time, there are many things that you can do to harass your illegal harassers.

First, of course, if they are seriously and illegally interfering with your rights as a citizen, without just cause, you can go to the courts and demand an injunction against the police department to force them to cease and desist.

However, this is a very difficult sort of legal case and not recommended except in the most extreme cases.

Ordinarily, it is more effective—and more fun—to harass the harassers.

The best way to do this is to put on a huge and phony "conspiracy" for the sleuths to track down.

Arrange lots of secret meetings with your associates in out-of-the-way places where it will be hard for the harassers to harass and talk a lot of gibberish and code words. Give them lots of nonsense to think about.

Don't overdo it, of course, or they will pay no attention.

One of the things I have done is to make a big show of sneaking somewhere near the police station, and then take out a pad and pencil and make drawings and plans of the buildings, with lots of dotted lines to various windows, etc.

Then tear off the drawings, AND LEAVE THE PAD WITH THE IMPRESSIONS ON IT behind.

You will have them sweating over this for quite some time if it is done with sufficient finesse and subtlety.

Many times, especially in the south, our people report they are being harassed by the "FBI." But when I investigate carefully, it turns out that the harassers are not the FBI at all, but unprofessional local detectives, working under political pressure from politicians who, in turn, are under pressure from the Jewish merchants who own the Main Streets of America.

How can you tell the difference between FBI agents and local detectives? Both often have something of the same appearance; both usually drive Fords, Chevys, or Plymouths with special equipment on the dashboard, travel in pairs, wear business suits with snap-brimmed hats, look sort of big and authoritative, and wear an indefinable look that reads "detective" unmistakably to any experienced observer.

To differentiate between FBI agents (who rarely act unprofessionally) and detectives (who often do), you have only to go down to the local federal building (usually the post office) and check the license plates of the Plymouths, Chevys, and Fords with no markings that are in the parking lot overnight. These will be FBI cars, and unless cars following you or harassing you have these license plates, you will know they are local detectives and not the FBI.

Time after time, I have found that especially southern patriots who have cursed the FBI for some unprofessional conduct have mistaken bullying local detectives for Bureau agents.

As I have said above, when Bureau agents get direct orders from the Jew Justice Department, or when they have reason to believe that a subject will commit a violent and illegal act, FBI agents will resort to "rough shadows" and harassment. But this is rare and usually justified by the "subject's" illegal conduct.

If you definitely identify the Bureau as the source of harassment, and you are innocent of any wrongdoing (as you should be if you are a member of this party or a student of this course), then I strongly suggest you go directly to the office of the Federal Bureau of Investigation in your area and ask to see the agent in charge.

If you "level" with him, act respectfully and responsibly, and offer to permit the Bureau to investigate anything they wish without warrants, so that you thoroughly convince him you are on the strict up-and-up (legally speaking), YOU WILL HAVE NO MORE TROUBLE WITH THE BUREAU.

Let me repeat, particularly to southern patriots, this will be hard to understand or believe, but it is true!

The Federal Bureau of Investigation knows for sure that I will be 100% open and above board with them, and they do not have to sneak around or harass me. They know I will not commit any bombings or illegal violence, nor permit such foolish actions, so they do not harass me or any of my people anywhere in the country. There is more I would like to say, but perceptive students will understand that I cannot.

My main point here is that there is absolutely no need for the insane battle between law-abiding southern patriots and the FBI.

Almost 100% of this childish hostility is caused by the attitude of many southern patriots, who completely fail to understand the function of the Federal Bureau of Investigation. The Bureau, by law, works for the Justice Department, which is almost 90% Jew and about 70% pro-Communist. The Justice Department is also about 200% in favor of race-mixing. Regardless of the personal sympathies of the agents, the Bureau is forced to obey orders. The alternative would be to resign their jobs, their income, their seniority, their retirement benefits, etc., etc.

And those who rage that "honest" agents should immediately resign rather than work for the Justice Department should recall the case of the great General Edwin Walker, who led the federal troops into Little Rock, and ordered the bayonets stuck in the backs of little White Christian girls to force mixing with niggers. General Walker did not believe in that any more than you or I, but he was a soldier and a good one, and he obeyed orders. So do the Bureau agents, the marshals, and the rest of the officers, including local detectives, with whom you will be dealing.

As I have pointed out in previous lessons, these people, by nature, are men of directness and force, and are psychologically on our side. If you give them half a chance, they will be "decent" to you. But if you snarl and snap at them, like a mad dog, they will be forced to TREAT you like a mad dog. Any human being resents offensive and aggressive conduct. And tough, hard-boiled FBI agents and detectives especially resent such snotty conduct.

So, I once again recommend that, if you determine that you are being harassed by the FBI, go directly to the agent in charge and establish warm personal contact.

I cannot emphasize strongly enough that if you do this sincerely and well, you will have no further trouble with the Bureau. The same goes for local police forces, although they are much more often unprofessional and under the direct influence of the Main Street Jew merchants.

If you run into unprofessional, illegal, and toadying local detectives, that is the time to use every stratagem and tactic taught herein to make it clear that you are not to be bullied, pushed around, or dealt with illegally in any manner.

Even with such police departments, especially in the South (and especially in ATLANTA, the Jew capital of the South), there is much to be gained by going directly to the top police officials and refusing to play their game of hide-and-seek or cops-and-robbers.

The Silent Shadow

If you ever discover that you are under very carefully disguised surveillance, so that you are sure they do not want you to know about it, never let the surveillants know that you know you are under surveillance!

As I have repeated over and over in this course, and in every other writing, you should be doing nothing illegal anyway.

On the other hand, in the legal fight for elective political power, you will often need to achieve legal and political SURPRISE. You may want to appear at a distant point somewhere without the knowledge of our opponents, or you may want to mount a demonstration for which you do not want them to have the chance to mount a counter-demonstration. Whatever the reason, there may be good cause to escape surveillance.

In this case, it is far better that the tail does not become the least bit suspicious that you are aware of his presence. If he becomes suspicious that you know, he will double and re-double his precautions that you do not "escape," whereas if he is certain you do not know you are being followed, he will sooner or later "slack off" enough for you to outwit him.

First, here are some ways you can determine for sure whether or not you are under silent surveillance.

If you are on foot and the surveillance is of a moderate degree and not too highly organized, the best check is a confederate who tails you along a pre-arranged route through a city at maximum distance. Such a confederate can easily observe anyone who is making all the twists and turns that you are.

But highly professional and well-organized surveillants will never be so obvious. They will use three or more different agents so that it is difficult to identify any particular person who is always with the subject.

One of the ways of spotting such professional and well-organized surveillance is, again, to have a confederate tailing you at a considerable distance on a pre-arranged route. When you are all set, you should have a second confederate slip you an envelope in a suspicious manner and "take off." You should then open the envelope, put the contents in a pocket—<u>and throw the envelope into a public trash basket</u>.

The tailing confederate should then <u>watch the trash basket</u>.

Whoever retrieves the envelope is at least one of the team tailing you, and by keeping an eye on him, you can spot the rest of the team, usually two more men (or women).

If you are in an automobile, and the surveillants are using old-fashioned, clumsy physical methods of actually following you, they will probably use three different cars with radios. Of course, one of the easiest ways to deal with this is to have a radio set of your own, tuned to the police frequency, if that is legal (which it usually is).

Such direct following will usually be done by three or more cars cutting in from side streets to relieve each other, so that you cannot see any particular car following you.

The best way to "lose" such surveillance is to drive out into <u>open</u> country, if this is possible, where it would be quite impossible for any vehicle to follow you any distance without becoming obvious.

However, depending on what is involved and whether they are tailing your car or you, another effective way of "losing" the tail, in a crowded city, is to have a confederate at one of the main doors of a large department store. Another man drives you, with the tail right behind, up to another door of the department store, and you jump out, rush into the department store, and "disappear" into the crowds, to emerge at the second door and hop in the confederate's car.

Once, when Philadelphia police were harassing me all over Washington, D. C., I ditched them by waiting until I was being followed by a car with only one detective. I then had my driver let me out into a crowd, and the single detective couldn't stop and follow me because of traffic.

The next section on surveillance sounds a little over dramatic, but it is useful nevertheless. That is the subject of disguise. I suggest you go to your library and get a book on the subject, since it is really an art. We have one officer in the party here who is something of an expert on this, which has proved very handy. By getting theatrical makeup called spirit gum and special theatrical hair, you can make up all sorts of beards, whiskers, etc., which are astoundingly effective.

One of the best ways to use disguise is not to put it on AFTER the political demonstration or whatever you do not wish to be followed from, but BEFORE. Particularly on a long-term operation, it is far better to become known <u>in disguise</u>, and then to depart without it. That way, you use your own face and appearance as a "disguise," and it is, of course, "perfect."

It may be hard to believe that you could become well-known politically and still use your own face as a disguise, but because of one specific technique of the Jews who control our media of information, it has worked for me for years.

While the entire Scotland Yard force was hunting me all over England, with a tremendous hue and cry in the press, on TV and the radio, the Jews would not permit a single decent, normal picture of me to be printed anywhere, so that all of England was looking for a "monster." I had entered perfectly legally and had every right to be there, yet, because of the Jewish hatred of anti-Communists, etc., everybody from the Queen on down was hunting me to throw me in jail and deport me. Yet I was able to ride around on London buses and in taxi cabs, sit quietly in Hyde Park, and generally take my ease all over London, even posing for photographs in front of Scotland Yard <u>without being recognized</u>!

You will find that this same thing applies to you. The Jews still believe in what they call "the silent treatment" and will either black you out of all news, in direct contravention of all their lies about "freedom of the press" and "liberty" and "honesty," etc., or they will print such lies and misleading photographs of you that you can operate quite easily in public without being recognized. This is one of the biggest helps the Jews have ever provided for me in our national and international operations. I am sure they will extend the same courtesy to any anti-Communist White Christian who tries to expose them.

One of the tricks the boys in England taught me was the use of the legal "roadblock."

When I had finished working with Colin Jordan to set up the World Union of National Socialists at a camp in the Cotswolds, right under the nose of Scotland Yard, and in spite of several searches of the camp by Scotland Yard, getting me out was something else again.

We did it with a decoy and a roadblock. First, we had a tall visitor who resembled me in build, rig himself up rather clumsily as a woman, get into a fast sports car, and dash out heading for London. The whole press corps and gangs of sleuths took up the chase. As the little red MG with the phony dame rounded a curve, a Landrover pulled out of a small country lane and "stalled" in an impassable section of the little dirt road. The whole pack of followers braked to skidding stops in clouds of dust. By the time the Landrover was pushed aside, the little red MG was racing toward London. And by the time the pack caught up with it, there was no dame—and, no me. I had walked out of the camp with my arm around one of the girls and singing "beer" songs—talking loudly of the jolly time we would have at a pub. We walked right past the whole gang of surveillants in this manner. I quietly got in an old car and left. Scotland Yard couldn't find me again until I was ready to leave England—more than a week!

It is important to remember that every word in this lesson is designed to help you only so long as you obey the law scrupulously. Thus, the only help offered here is to those who are being illegally, unlawfully, and unfairly harassed, rather than those who are under legitimate surveillance, etc.

If you are full of love for our Constitution and our American traditions, for the White Race and for Western Christian civilization, you may be sure you will be banned (as I am from almost every country in the world), you will be harassed and hounded unmercifully, as I have been and as most patriots have also been. Nothing in this whole course should be interpreted as a method of defeating law enforcement officers or investigative officers in achieving legitimate ends. This course is to help you protect your Constitutional rights to privacy, to political freedom, to religious freedom, and freedom from unprofessional, bullying police departments under the domination of un-American, pro-Communist, and pro-race-mixing Jews and pinkos.

If you are alone and desire to watch behind you without such observation being apparent, you can, of course, use the old expedient of watching reflections in store windows. But this is much less effective than using the new "one-way" sunglasses, the kind that look like mirrors on the front. You can learn to use these as "rear view mirrors" so that you can stand or sit reading a paper and watch everything directly behind you.

Here are some methods by which you can harass harassers who are tailing you to illegally deprive you of your right to political association, privacy, etc. A phony "squealer" is very effective, provided he or she is really subtle and clever.

You can arrange a big "split" with suitable charges and counter-charges, etc., and then have your "enemy" "expose" you to the harassers.

If you discover that you are under surveillance by a spy in your organization, never let him become aware that you know he is a phony!

On the subject of counter-surveillance, let me warn all students and party members that it is illegal in many places to maintain any sort of private surveillance without a license. Be sure to look into the laws and regulations in your area before attempting any such thing. It is also illegal everywhere to usurp police powers or attempt in any way to act the part of a police officer. Don't do it!

On the other hand, there are literally thousands of ways to learn information about a suspected spy, Communist or other enemy of our Republic and the White Christian people who built it, without breaking the law.

The first method is research. The novice in this business is always amazed by the number of sources of information about individuals' private lives without any actual surveillance.

First, there are the credit agencies. If you own a business, or have a friend who does or who is a lawyer, you can ask for the Dunn & Bradstreet or other credit reports and character reports on a subject.

You can go to the library and check city directories, business directories, such as *Standard & Poor's*, *Moody's*, etc., "Who's Who" directories for the world, the country, and sometimes special groups. The Jews, until 1956, published *Who's Who in American Jewry*. But then, too many of us were using this gold mine of facts to expose the fantastic rate at which hell-raising, disloyal, communistic, and Zionist Jews are seizing business and political control of the United States, so they stopped publishing the book.

They still publish *Who's Who in World Jewry*; however, it is still available in England, I believe. And there are plenty of other business and professional directories and directories of various ethnic groups in which you can look up the basic background facts of many prominent individuals.

To anti-Communists, perhaps the most valuable single research source is a set of three volumes put out by the House Committee on Un-American Activities and called *Appendix IX*.

This fantastic set of three books is a compilation of documents, exhibits, and facts about hundreds and hundreds of Communist-front organizations, with the names, addresses, and facts of the participants therein.

A vast proportion of these Communist rats, as a perusal of the *Appendix* will show, are open Jews. Many of these Communists, who have changed their names, are exposed for their true Jewish origin, with their Yiddish name.

For this reason, as might be easily imagined, *Appendix IX* is "out of print" at the Government Printing Office, and for years was absolutely "unattainable." The Jews don't like it.

Finally, some patriots in California had it reprinted, and it can be obtained from Poor Richard's Book Shop, 5403 Hollywood Blvd., Los Angeles 27, California. Counting postage, the cost is $ 29.90.

Although the Jews stopped all such information after 1946 or '47, whenever there is suspected Communist and treasonable race-mixing activity in your area, you can always pick up this *Appendix IX*, look in the index, and find some of the older race-mixing agitators and Red rats listed therein.

This *Appendix IX* is also fabulous for the way it exposes

many phony "anti-Communists" presently being fobbed off on us as "experts" on the Communist menace. (The Overstreets are a good example of this, being the authors of several actual TEXTBOOKS used in schools in learning how to fight Communism, although you will often find the Overstreets listed in Communist-front groups. *Appendix IX.*)

Let me caution all students and responsible right-wingers against the miserable failure of too many of us to "do our homework." Never refer to any suspected individual as a "Jew" or "Communist" unless you KNOW, from unimpeachable sources, that the subject is, indeed, a Jew. Too many right-wingers simply read that so-and-so is a "Communist Jew" in some other irresponsible right-wing paper, and thereupon take it for gospel fact. Then still other patriots read it in the second guy's publication and consider it thoroughly "proved," since it has been printed twice. Before too long, it is part of right-wing dogma, and any questioning of the "fact" is considered "treason."

What these irresponsible people forget is that in approaching intelligent people with the claim that we are fighting for "the truth" (which we are), our whole strength and hope lies in TELLING THE TRUTH. When we tell a big, fat, easily disproved, and stupid LIE, we completely discredit the hundreds of thousands of deadly facts we must get to the American people.

Too many right-wingers spend their time talking, writing, speaking, and circulating only among other right-wingers. They thus have no idea how such a blatant lie completely smashes an otherwise beautiful job of winning over intelligent and responsible young people.

I am very successfully speaking at colleges and universities all over America all the time. And I can assure party members and students that nothing would make it so easy for Jews, Communists, and nigger hecklers to smash me as to be able to expose me before a vast audience for telling one whopping lie, such as that Nicholas Katzenbach, "the nigger-loving Attorney General, is a "Jew."

In short, the right-wing "gets away" with its sloppy or nonexistent research only because it almost never goes among the enemy, as we do all the time in winning youth.

It is presumed that our members and students of this course want to win, not just circulate amongst other right-wingers. And nothing is so sure to prevent our victory as stupid, easily disproved lies.

Don't make the mistake of originating such suicidal lies, nor of spreading the foolish lies of other lazy right-wingers who do not do their "homework." Do your research "homework."

To sum up this lesson, I must again repeat, (1) be sure to stay legal! Do not break the law. Before you do anything recommended in this lesson, check the laws and regulations in the area in which you are operating, and (2) be professional!

If police are operating professionally and lawfully, and you find yourself being followed, it is usually best to pay no attention whatsoever. They won't bother you. If possible, and the tail stays with you over a long period of time, try to make friends with him and even show him small, thoughtful courtesies. (Once, in Florida, when I was inside a lovely home as a guest at dinner, while the detectives sat outside, hiding in their car, hungry, I took them out some paper plates of dinner which they couldn't resist—and they both felt pretty guilty about following me around.)

When you first start operating in any area, party members and students should go directly to the offices of the FBI in the area and to the Chief of Police, the District Attorney, etc., and forthrightly, courteously, and without any arrogance or smugness, inform the authorities of your intention to conduct a legal campaign against Jewish Communism, Jewish race-mixing, Zionism, and all other forms of treason and subversion of our White Christian American Constitutional Republic. If you believe in the methods taught in this course, you will NOT sneak. You will have nothing to hide (except an occasional tactical "surprise" on a political demonstration—which is perfectly legal).

Above all, you will become and remain a PROFESSIONAL.

To learn more precisely what I mean by that term, observe the manner of most state police officers and most FBI agents. I might also add that most local police officers and detectives in all but a few Jewish-dominated big cities like Philadelphia are also professional and ethical.

When you run into a situation where officials are NOT professional and ethical, don't make the mistake of acting "wise" or in any manner like a hoodlum.

You are a PROFESSIONAL. You would not have taken this course otherwise. Your "business" is the survival of our White Western Constitutional form of government! Your business is not fighting policemen, showing them how "clever" you are, or being "tough." Your business is WINNING!

And to win victory over the most vicious and deadly conspiracy in the history of the world, you are going to have to be what is termed in the vernacular, "sharp." You are going to have to be calm, self-reliant, smooth, sure, completely well-informed, self-controlled, quietly courageous—and, above all—LEGAL!

LESSON NO. 3

Test Questions

1. Why should you always conduct yourself in such a manner that tapes or films of your words and actions would not embarrass you in court?

2. How can a person be overheard in a room containing no "bugs" or microphones?

3. Is conversation in an automobile while driving "safe" from being overheard? Explain.

4. How can you tell for SURE whether or not your automobile is under surveillance?

5. What is the best single device for ensuring privacy of conversation between two people?

6. What are two things you can do to help stop an illegal police "harassment" by "rough shadow"?

7. Name one advantage to a party member or student of being under FBI surveillance.

8. In what one legal situation is it necessary and proper for party members and students to escape surveillance?

9. What small device is helpful in throwing a pack of foot surveillants off balance? How should it be used?

10. List the steps in counter-harassing a pack of illegal, harassing detectives, without breaking the law.

11. What can you do to embarrass and shame a pack of police cars and detective cars who are illegally harassing you and depriving you of your right to privacy with no cause?

12. Describe one method of "ditching a tail."

13. How can you tell the difference between FBI vehicles and detective cars?

14. Although their goal of protecting our White Christian American Constitutional Republic from Communist, Zionist, and nigger traitors is commendable, why are the tactics of the southern bombers and terrorists absolutely wrong?

15. Give one way to discover if you are being followed by a well-organized, professional group.

16. What is the best method to "force the hand" of clumsy automobile surveillants?

17. What is the best way to lose a tail in a big city?

18. What one tactic of the Jews is especially helpful to us?

19. What is a more effective way than watching reflections in store windows to observe what is going on behind you?

20. What is the best source of information on the background of older, suspected pro-Communists in race-mixing, peace creep, or other disloyal demonstrations?

21. Name one way of obtaining personal information on a subject without surveillance.

22. What are the two cardinal rules of all our tactical operations?

23. What British publication will help identify Communist-Jews, in foreign countries?

24. Why is it so necessary to make sure you do not lie or make false statements about the enemy?

25. When are you justified in harassing those who are subjecting you to a "rough shadow"?

26. What is the name of one confidential report you can get through a lawyer or businessman?

27. How should you act toward a "silent shadow" of which you are aware but which is causing you no difficulty?

28. When you are sure one of your group is a "rat," what is the best way to identify him?

29. Should you always expel a spy once you have identified him?

30. Should you beat him up? Explain.

LESSON NO. 4
Cross-Examination

In fighting Jewish Communism, Zionism, and race mixing, you will rarely face any danger as deadly as a LYING WITNESS.

If you do more than talk, and actually get out there and demonstrate and stand up for your race and nation, as you should, it is inevitable that you will be charged by craven, nigger-and-Jew-loving politicians with everything from treason and declarations of war (we have been charged with both of these) to "littering the street" and "loitering."

None of these charges is worth a nickel—unless they are backed up by liars on the witness stand.

My experience has been that very, very few cops will get up there and lie. It has happened to me only once, but I was fortunate to have a motion picture that refuted the perjury by the cop, and it happened only that one time. The rest of the time, even nigger cops have not lied.

Most ordinary coons are too dumb to dare lie in a courtroom.

But Christ and a lot of other experts called the Jews "the great Masters of the Lie," and I can assure you that these experts were 100% right. As much as you may already know about the Jews behind Communism, race-mixing, and Zionist treason, you will nevertheless get a cold shock the first time you see and hear some of these creatures up there on a witness stand. Their impudence in telling the most fantastic lies, with tears pouring down both sides of their Jew noses, is absolutely incredible! You have to hear it to believe it!

Usually, they throw in a heart-rending story of how their poor, dear old mother was gassed two or three times in Belsen, Majdanek, Auschwitz, etc., while they themselves were also gassed at least once a week.

The power of the Jews being what it is, now as in the time of Christ (when "He would not walk in Jewry for fear of the Jews"), judges will almost universally pitch in and help the Hebrews with this sniveling act and give a speech about "Hitler's gas ovens," etc.

But it is not just the phony, tear-jerking scene that is most dangerous to you.

The Jews are unbelievable experts at telling a harrowing story of how they innocently came down the street, saw a commotion, and there YOU were—beating on these poor, defenseless Jews—thousands of them!

After some demonstration, in which huge mobs of Jews have attacked our pickets, I have been forced to sit in a courtroom for hours listening to a whole parade of these world's champion liars take turns swearing under oath that we attacked them!!

Of course, as we will cover later in the lesson on picketing, the best defense against these unspeakable perjurers is a camera, preferably a movie camera. You should always try your best to have a cameraman record all demonstrations where an attack by Jewish "love-mongers" is likely. But once the Jews get wise to this precaution, they will often attack the cameraman first, if they can find him. (We usually try to place him in an upstairs window, if possible, for this reason.)

If you have a photographic record of the action, it is well to let the Jews go ahead and put on their "He-sniff-sniff-beat-me!" act and then show your movies. Even the most Jew-loving judge in the world will be repelled by photographic evidence of the Jew's arrogance in lying. (Although we have never been able to get these chosen ones nailed for their perjury.)

However, if you are hauled into court after being attacked by a mob of Jews, or if you are facing any other charges and you face a perjured witness, your only real, sure defense is cross-examination.

Whenever a witness has been brought forward by the prosecution against you, they must give you the absolute right to try your best, by all legal means, to show that he is either lying or doesn't know what he is talking about.

There are two ways you can do this: (1) you can "impeach" him as a person—that is, you can prove that his record of crime and perjury and immorality is so bad that anything he says is highly suspect; or (2) you can make him "impeach" himself by contradicting himself or the facts. Basically, those are the only two things you can do to a witness to break down the damaging testimony he has given against you.

To make use of the first method (to impeach a witness), you must know something of his background. You must know, for sure, that he is a criminal, a perjurer, an immoral wretch of some kind, or is otherwise unworthy of belief by the judge and/or jury. If you have such information, you simply have to present it to him and ask him if it is true, etc. Get him to identify and introduce into the record any documents of arrests, convictions, etc., that you can obtain. Get him to admit his whole past record, and remember, he

MUST answer. Don't let them soft-soap or buffalo you out of your right to "impeach" an enemy witness. You have the absolute right to do this. You do not have the right to "bully" a witness and should almost never raise your voice or act like some kind of TV courtroom hero. But you must gently and firmly insist on your right to bring out the most unsavory things you KNOW about a witness against you. Don't go "fishing," hoping to find something derogatory. This is illegal and will hurt your cause, besides. But if you have something on him, throw it right in his lap and then make him eat it right before the jury. The more he tries to squirm out of it, the better for you.

Usually, however, we are far too poor and hard-pressed to be able to dig up or find out such past misbehavior by witnesses against us. We have to take them as they come at us, right there on the spot.

There is a scientific, sure way to smash to bits the calculating liar on the witness stand, and it is the main burden of this lesson to teach you that scientific method of destroying perjurers in open court.

Unless you can do this, you are almost helpless in court, no matter how much other procedure you know. Perjury is relatively rare in most courts. Most people don't consciously lie, but are simply hazy in their memories or guilty of wishful thinking. But in OUR cases, especially street cases involving Jews, perjury is the iron-clad rule, and you will face masters of the art almost every time.

There are only two basic ways to expose these liars in open court under cross-examination: (1) get the witness to swear to two mutually contradictory statements, and the jury will see for themselves that the Jew is lying; or (2) show that he has lied about some easily proven fact. There are literally thousands of ways of doing these two things.

However, the student should remember that there are still only TWO ways to go after an enemy witness: (1) impeach his character and record; or (2) prove he is a liar, by getting him to swear to two mutually contradictory statements, one of which must be a lie, or by swearing to a fact which is false.

Fundamentally, the basic method of countering perjurers revolves around the word "DETAILS."

Whenever you are suddenly faced with the task of cross-examination and have had no time to prepare and plan, remember that key word, "DETAILS!"

Here's why.

Think of dinner last night. In most cases, you will have trouble recalling what you ate, where you ate it, with whom you ate it, what you talked about, etc.

Suppose you are on the witness stand today and testify that I was there at the table and suggested we all go out and rob a bank. If it is true, and I DID this, and I WAS at the table with you—you will have no trouble answering the most minute details of what was eaten, etc.

But now, let's make a liar out of you. Let's put you back on the stand under oath before all those people looking at you, with the judge glaring down at you from the bench, and have you claim that you ate dinner at MY house last night, and I suggested we rob a bank, after which we went to a movie.

Quick, now, can you tell me what was served? Where? Where did I sit? Where did you sit? Who else was there? What time? Did you hear anything? What was I eating when the suggestion was made? What was I wearing? Was my dog in the room? What kind of dog is he? Was he well-behaved? Did we feed him anything? Where were you before we had dinner together? What movie did we see? What theater? When?

Do you see that it might be difficult to answer those questions?

Now add another element.

While you are answering those rapid-fire questions from a cross-examiner, let us presume he is carefully noting down all your answers on a little pad. You can see him doing it.

Now, after about an hour of asking you all the details about that dinner, he goes back and starts asking some of the same questions again, this time in a different order. Where did you say you sat? Did you say they did or did not serve rolls? Where did other people sit? Left? Right? Who was on whose right? Time? How do you know? Etc.

The lying witness, seeing the cross-examiner checking all these answers on his little pad, will get more and more nervous, especially if the cross-examiner gives some well-played little signs of satisfaction at contradictions, clucks over mistakes, notes confusion down, etc. Sooner or later, the liar will bust, bust wide open, and protest that he can't "remember" all that stuff, etc. That's the time to ask how, then, how can he be so sure of the facts which might send you to the jug?

When you know you are going to be confronted by such a liar, or a parade of liars, you usually also know pretty well what they are going to come on with.

I suggest you sit down quietly, before the trial, and make out a very extensive checklist of details. If possible, check some of the facts. For instance, if it is street action involved, measure the sidewalk. Often, the Jews will get up there and swear they were blocked from passing along the sidewalk, and that is why they "had to" attack us. Check the number of passersby at the same general time every day as the incident. Check the various angles of vision, the light, the weather, the number of police usually in the area, etc. But you should also include in your list such things as "clothes," "other people," etc.—every conceivable circumstance present at the scene. A truthful person might have to think hard to recall all the answers, but they could usually do it. A liar, on the other hand, will be painfully confused and scared when you start asking details in an organized, ruthless but quiet manner.

If there is some key fact involved in the case, such as the amount of light by which the witness says he observed the crime, etc.—check all the key facts. The classic case of Abraham Lincoln's, in which he got a witness to explain how he saw all the gory details of the crime by moonlight, after which Lincoln produced the Almanac to show there was NO moon that night, is perhaps the best example.

And whenever you have a "trap" like this to spring, never make the mistake of doing it prematurely.

Lead the witness to "dig himself in" good and solid in his lies. Ask him several times, even if it brings objections, if he is sure he saw thus and so. Get him aggravated so he really drives it in hard.

Then, gently, with no flourish or braggadocio, "bomb" him with the truth. Quietly present him with the photo, the book, the map, or whatever it is that will destroy him. Let him "blow up" all alone, for the full benefit of the jury. Don't make the mistake of gloating. As soon as you are sure your victim is "dead" with the jury, mercifully turn him loose and show no sign of "triumph."

With Jew perjurers, there is something else you can use to expose them as liars.

Most of them are so damnably subjective and arrogant that they overreach themselves, even in a courtroom.

When you get up to cross-examine one of them, he will turn upon you such a look of burning hate and villainy that you will know he is halfway to madness already. They preach "love," but they so viciously hate anybody who exposes their activities that they can't hide it.

With such raging, Jewy, pulpy-nosed Israeli types, I have been quite successful with the following approach.

Q. Are you Jewish?

A. Yes, I'm Jewish, and proud of it! We Jews have done much for the world!

Q. Are you a "Nazi"?

A. Am I a NAZI? A NAZI? You are asking me am I a NAZI? You crazy? Am I a Nazi!

Q. Yes, sir. Are you a Nazi?

A. I refuse to answer any such insane question. You know what I think of Nazis!

Q. No, sir. What do you think of Nazis?

A. Nazis are devils! They are full of hate! You Nazis helped kill six million people, Rockwell! You are murderers, killers, you ought to be put away someplace! (Raging) I'd like a chance to...

Q. Excuse me, sir, would you please just answer the questions? Do you dislike Nazis?

A. Dislike Nazis?! DisLIKE! I,---I,---I, I HATE Nazis!

Q. Do you think Nazis ought to be stopped?

A. "Stopped" isn't the word for it. They ought to be hung, all of them! Just give me ten minutes alone in a room with you, Rockwell, and I'd show you ...

COURT: Just a minute, Mr. Blatzhitz, hold it. The court understands how you feel and sympathizes, but you must not make speeches—just answer the questions.

Q. I'm interested in what this witness was saying, Your Honor. What would you do to me, sir?

A. I'd break your rotten neck for you, Rockwell, that's what I'd do! I---I-I-I---d, --

COURT: Mr. Blatzhitz, MR. BLATZHITZ!

A. Yes, Your Honor. I'm sorry, Your Honor, but I couldn't help it. This vile Rockwell is --I'd just like..."

Q. Would you like to punch me, Mr. Blatzhitz?

A. Punch you! Punch you wouldn't be the half of it!

Q. Just because I'm a "Nazi," would you like to see me in jail?

A. Jail is where you should be! You should be dead!

Q. Would you go out of your way to put us Nazis in jail?

A. I'd do anything I could to put scum like you in jail where you belong.

Q. Anything, Mr. Blatzhitz?

A. Anything!

Q. Would you come down here to this courtroom, Mr. Blatzhitz, and tell these ladies and gentlemen of the jury that I hit those old Jews with a stick—if you knew it would send me to jail?

After all this, the jury will have no trouble seeing the fires of raging, burning, and devilish hate motivating the Jew witness, and they will feel with their hearts the Jewish viciousness which makes them the liars and devils Christ called them. Their Jewish hate-testimony will be useless.

There is a more subtle way you can sometimes discredit these Jew fakers.

Reuben Garland of Atlanta is the greatest criminal lawyer I have ever met. He has saved dozens of murderers from the chair and is a master courtroom performer of the old style.

When five of our lads were on trial in Atlanta for dynamiting a synagogue, the rabbi's wife got up and testified that George Bright, one of the accused "bombers," had called her and threatened her. Mr. Garland first cross-examined the rabbi's wife on her background, and established, for the benefit of the Georgia jury, that this lady had formerly been a dance-hall performer from NEW YORK CITY.

Mr. Garland asked how the Jewess was able to know who was threatening her.

A. I knew his voice. I recognized his voice. It was Mr. Bright.

Q. How did you recognize his voice, if you didn't know him?

A. I recognized it by the quality and pitch.

Q. But it might have been lots of people; how do you know it was this defendant?

A. Well, by his accent.

Q. His ACCENT? What accent?

A. Well, he has a -- he talks different.

Q. How do you mean?

A. His ACCENT.

Q. But what KIND of an accent does he have?

A. Well, he talks like one of these Southern people; he has an ignorant Southern accent.

Q. An "IGNORANT, SOUTHERN accent"—is that how you New York folks recognize Georgia people?

And Mr. Garland had no more trouble with that jury.

I could go on for a long time with all sorts of different tricks and anecdotes. But I think it would be a waste of time to proliferate examples.

The only way I can help the student is to teach him principles, and let him then mold his own examples from the basic principles.

And the basic principle is to make an enemy witness either a LIAR OR A LOUSE.

If you possibly can, expose him as a big, bare-faced liar.

If this is impossible, your only recourse is to show that he is a louse.

To expose him as a liar, you must either catch him in self-contradictions or catch him falsifying provable facts.

To expose him as a louse, you need background information. You can also appeal to any local sentiment that may be against the witness. Admittedly, this latter course is "irrational." But they do it to us, and the object in court is to survive, not teach Sunday school.

Knowing what not to do in cross-examination is almost as important as knowing what you should do.

There are two situations in which you absolutely should NOT cross-examine, as we mentioned in the first lesson.

If the witness against you is a woman or a child, it will take masterful control to cross-examine with benefit to your side, and the chances are at least 50-50 that you will stumble into a very painful and perhaps fatal situation.

When the witness is a woman or child, you must be extremely careful to give no impression of bullying or high pressure. This is especially true before a jury. Most judges realize your difficult situation and may possibly make an allowance for it. But a jury has a tremendous built-in (and natural) prejudice in favor of women and children (especially as a Nazi), and they will be at least a little bit hostile toward you.

For these reasons, you should approach women and children on the witness stand with the utmost solicitation and courtesy. It does not hurt to bend far over backward to be thoughtful, gentle, humble, and even apologetic.

Regardless of the vicious nature of some of the Jewish and other females you may encounter in these situations, you should give the impression of one who is deeply pained at the necessity to subject the "lady" to such a brutal experience as this cross-examination, and you should say almost exactly this before commencing the cross-examination. You should make it clear to the jury, in explaining to the witness, that you have no choice and that you are on trial for your liberty (or life), and it will therefore be necessary to cross-examine, but you intend to do it as gently and "painlessly" as possible. The technique you use should then be aimed at doing precisely this.

In the course of your questioning (liberally interlarded with apologies and solicitous statements of concern for the tender feelings of the witness), you should gently lead the witness into a situation in which she (or the child) WILL DISCREDIT HERSELF.

Do not make the fatal mistake of bullying or crowing over her (or the child) even then—at least not prematurely.

If and when you have been totally successful in leading the witness to completely discredit and expose herself as a liar and a vicious person to the jury, then, and only then, can you use "rubbing-it-in" tactics, if these seem called for and effective.

However, I recommend abstaining altogether and allowing the false witness to withdraw from the stand, a "fallen woman" thoroughly discredited by her own answers, despite the utmost courtesy and gentle approach on your part.

At this point, I should like to remind the student again that, just as in salesmanship, a very large percentage of success depends on your ability to make the jury LIKE you, so that they will transfer emotional "favoritism" to your cause and reasoning. That is the basic reason for being so gentle with witnesses who are female or underage, etc.

If there is any question in your mind about your ability to lead the female or child witness gently to utter discreditation, don't cross-examine. It would be almost fatal to get up there and "dally around" with such a witness, only to have her emerge completely "pure" and unexposed. It makes you look like a dishonorable, ungentlemanly, and bullying villain trying to "take advantage" of the "poor, defenseless lady."

There is another situation in which you absolutely must not cross-examine. Whenever the facts which have been brought out by a witness against you are TRUE, and they are very damaging, and there is no way you can discredit or impeach the witness or his character, you should "take your medicine" and get on to something else as quickly as possible.

I have seen one amateur after another completely ruin any chances he might have had by insisting on cross-examining a witness against whom he had no chance whatsoever. When an unimpeachable witness has testified that you did something criminal or incriminating, and he has made a strong impression on the jury, if you then get up to cross-examine, all you will do is reinforce, in the minds of the jury, the already strong impression against you.

Perhaps the most stupid and suicidal question ever heard in any courtroom is the defendant who gets up and asks a police witness against him, "Are you then saying that you saw me hit that Jew with a club?"

The policeman then replies "Yes, sir, you hit him twice"— or some similar statement which actually ADDS to the evidence against you, and is twice as damaging when you yourself brought it out.

In short, NEVER CROSS-EXAMINE WHEN YOU ARE SURE YOU CAN NOT BREAK EITHER THE WITNESS OR HIS TESTIMONY!

Finally, there is yet one more situation in which you should never cross-examine. If a witness testifies to a fact that does not in any way damage you, just let him go. If you wish, and you are capable of effective theatrics, when the prosecution offers a witness to you for cross-examination, you may, in such cases, magnanimously wave the witness away with a sort of cheerful "No questions!" which sounds a subtle note of triumph to the jury, which they may remember later when you put on your own case.

A good example of this occurred when the "courthouse gang" in Jew- and nigger-dominated Emporia, Virginia, tried to charge me with "starting a war against the Negro people in Virginia."

One of the Witnesses brought forth by the prosecution was a man who testified to having seen two guns lying on the seat of my automobile. The prosecuting attorney made a big deal of these guns and had the witness describe them in all their ferocious details.

I am sure that everybody in the courtroom expected me to try to do something about this "incriminating" development.

Instead, I actually smiled and very subtly did my best to indicate a sort of scornful pity for the prosecutor.

The facts were that it is not only not illegal to carry unconcealed pistols in Virginia, but that I had taken the extra precaution of writing to the Chief of the State Police a notice of my intention to carry these particular pistols. I had given him the serial numbers thereof and assured him of my intention to use them only for purposes of defense if necessary. I had in the courtroom my letter from him acknowledging my letter and the legality of my procedure.

I could have brought this all out right after the testimony about the pistols, but it was much more effective to let it appear that they "had" me cold and let this false impression get built up into a big thing before I knocked it down by introducing my letter from the Chief of the State Police into evidence. The prosecutor and the courthouse gang were demolished in this attempt to make it look as though my two pistols were the first signs of my coming "war" against the niggers of Virginia.

We now come to the subject of how to handle yourself under cross-examination by the enemy.

The first thing to remember, especially for those who are unfamiliar with these situations, is never to permit yourself to be bullied or pushed into rushing!

You have a duty on the witness stand to answer questions honestly and truthfully. You have no duty to answer them instantly. Prosecutors are usually thoroughly familiar with courtroom procedure and are quite at ease, while you will often be uneasy, worried, scared, and fearfully nervous, regardless of your innocence.

Under these circumstances, if you are not extremely careful, you can be hurried and harried into answering a machine gun-like series of rapid-fire questions, which lead you into a fatal trap.

YOU HAVE THE ABSOLUTE RIGHT TO TAKE SUFFICIENT TIME TO REFLECT BEFORE ANSWERING EACH AND EVERY QUESTION.

The moment a prosecutor starts the machine gun approach, no matter how nervous you are, consciously and forcefully pause and think before answering each and every question, no matter how simple. His technique will be to fire a series of easy and non-incriminating questions at you to get you answering almost instantly without thinking, and then start throwing devilishly loaded questions at you, and when you get confused and pause, to use the result to imply to the jury that you are lying and trying to "cover up."

Therefore, never let him get started on this attack. Answer each and every question, no matter how simple, slowly and deliberately. Later, when you become thoroughly at ease and an expert in this juridical swordplay, you can afford to thrust and parry with lightning speed and clever ripostes. But until you are completely sure of yourself and a master of the situation, I recommend that our people make an unvarying habit of answering ALL questions slowly and deliberately.

If the prosecutor bullies and harasses you and gets you upset, turn to the judge and very respectfully ask for help from him. If you do this correctly, you will not only get the help, even if the judge is a Jew (because it is his duty and any other course would show him up as a louse)—but you will win much sympathy from the jury who can easily imagine themselves sitting on your hot spot and facing that yapping prosecutor.

Remember that when you are questioning your own witnesses under direct examination, it is illegal for you to ask "leading" questions. You cannot ask questions requiring a "Yes" or "No" answer.

But in cross-examination, you are permitted to "hypothesize." You can ask, for instance, "Is it not true that you went down to that theater to start a riot and get the Nazis thrown in jail?"

This is a terrific weapon if used intelligently and carefully.

I have found it is not so good in forcing a witness to admit "Yes" answers to such questions as the above, as it is in throwing the witness off the track and provoking him into telling the truth you want brought out.

For instance, when you know that the Jews came down to your picket or speech, etc., specifically to start a riot and get you and your group jailed (which is their almost invariable pattern of operation), you can use the "loaded" and leading question permitted by cross-examination to mislead the witness as to your real intentions and get him to burst out with the truth.

As an example, you could ask the Jew witness, after you have got him stirred up and emotional, "Is it not true that you were paid cash money to go down there to that picket?" "No!" he will explode, and before he has the words fully out, you come back with, "Is it not true you were paid $50 apiece to come down there and start that riot?"

Again, he will roar "No," and you can keep up such a barrage of questions implying that he was PAID to do what you know he did but won't admit. He will get so outraged at this implication of "commercialism" that he will often burst out with the fact that he roundly hates you and everything you stand for and went down to start that riot to get you put in jail, etc.—and that's precisely what you were after in the first place. When you get it, point out the fact to the jury, thank the witness with mock gratitude, and retire to your seat.

Another technique, which is effective and legal in cross-examination, is to get the witness to keep enlarging on his position little by little until it becomes grossly ridiculous and obvious to the jury.

This is particularly effective with these Jew preachers of "love" and "tolerance." If the judge permits questions in the field of ideology and beliefs (which they usually don't), you may use the occasion to expose the Jews for the hypocrites and liars they are by misleading your kike witness gently and carefully in denouncing "Nazism" for being full of "hate," etc., and from there generally denouncing ALL "hate."

You can then start asking the Jew questions whether he would hate a man who banged his fender on a city street. He is able to answer "NO" to this. Then you start increasing the offense of the other person against the Jew until you wind up with Adolf Hitler and the phony six million Jews, etc., at which point the Jew will usually start raging that such monsters as Nazis deserve to be "hated" and that he does, indeed, hate them with a passion.

In closing this lesson, let me do all within my power to motivate the student to expend more time and effort on the subject of cross-examination than was involved in this lesson. There are good books on this one subject in all law libraries and many general libraries. You should get some of them and read them. They contain hundreds of examples of magnificent cross-examination techniques. (Two books on this subject, which nearly all legal libraries have, are: *The Art of Cross-Examination* by Francis L. Wellman, N. Y., Macmillan Co., 1953; and *Argument* by Harold F. Graves, N. Y., Cordon Co., 1938.) Many of these books are by brilliant and clever Jews. You should learn their "dirty tricks" and be ready to apply them as necessary in the courtroom.

And, above all, never forget that your first and foremost defense against the perjured witnesses we almost always face in court is DETAILS.

Whenever an enemy witness is testifying, do not waste any time or effort gasping or making faces when he tells lies to show the jury that he is a liar, etc. Watch him carefully and make accurate notes of precisely what he says, and remember DETAILS.

When you get your chance to cross-examine, get him to tell hundreds of other details. While you are doing this, you must "think on your feet" and be searching for and organizing all contradictions in the details the liar invents. Inevitably, there will be many contradictions. Once you have found a big one, start beating him over the head with it, and he will make one slip after another, and you can wind up utterly destroying him with his own testimony.

You will find this one skill to be your single most valuable technical asset in fighting the Jew, Communist, Zionist race-mixing liars you will face in court year after year.

This is something you can actually practice on your associates. Have one man invent a lying story about you, then you cross-examine him on the details. Have him try his very best to keep straight, while you keep doggedly after him until you catch him in inconsistencies and build these until you have utterly destroyed his story. Practice until you are an expert at this technique.

One day, it may very well save you from years in the penitentiary.

LESSON NO. 4
Test Questions

1. Innocent Nazis can be convicted and sent to jail if they do not know how to cope with __________ witnesses against them in court.

2. Policemen who are witnesses in court will (always,never, rarely) tell lies on the witness stand.

3. History has proven that the most clever and convincing liars on earth are (the Negroes, the Jews, the judges, the police).

4. Even though some judges fall for the Jews' lies, a Nazi on trial can win his freedom by exposing the Jews' perjury to the ______________________.

5. The only real, sure defense a Nazi in court has against a perjured witness is______________________.

6. What are the two ways to "impeach" a witness?

7. A person who is defending himself in court on a criminal charge and who is inexperienced in court procedures does not have the right to "impeach" a witness. (True or False?)

8. It is illegal and harmful to attempt to impeach a witness on his past record if the cross-examiner does not really know <u>facts</u> about the witness which would make him unbelievable by a judge and jury. (True or False?)

9. Of the two methods of exposing a liar on the witness stand, which is the one most readily available to Nazis?.

10. Perjury by a Jew witness in court is (rare, normal) when a Nazi is on trial.

11. What are the two ways to expose liars under cross-examination?

12. The one most important thing to remember in cross-examining a witness suspected of being a liar, is to ask him plenty of _________________.

13. One advantage a cross-examiner has over a witness is that the cross-examiner can ________ ________ the witness's answers, but the witness can't.

14. Is it better to think up all the details to ask a witness under cross-examination before the trial begins, or while you are on your feet, doing the questioning? Why?

15. The best way to conduct oneself while defending oneself in court is to shout at the witness, trying to catch him in a lie. (True or False?)

16. When a Jew witness is lying, he is arrogant and self-assured about <u>big</u> things, but gets nervous and scared when pinned down on ___________________.

17. If a cross-examiner knows of a key fact the witness is lying about, what should he do to the witness before "springing the trap"?

18. In questioning witnesses and going through other courtroom procedures, one should never forget that everything he does or says is calculated to impress (the judge, the jury, the press).

19. What characteristic of Jews can sometimes be exploited to render a lying Jew witness's testimony useless?

20. While developing a Jew witness's downfall through the method referred to in Question No. 19, which attitude should the cross-examiner assume during the questioning? a) Utter contempt for the Jew; b) Highly emotional; c) Arrogance; d) Disrespect; e) Threatening; f) Calm, collected, and respectful; g) Gleeful.

21. The surest way of saving yourself in court is to show that an enemy witness is a __________ . What two ways are there to do this?

22. Besides showing the jury that an enemy witness is a liar, what is the next best thing to bring out about him? How is this done?

23. What is the main reason for being super-courteous and "nice" when questioning a witness who is a woman or a child?

24. If the witness you are cross-examining is a Jewish woman who obviously hates you, it is not necessary to be gentle and humble in questioning her. (True or False?) Why?

25. In questioning a woman witness, the main object in your behaving in an apologetic and solicitous manner is to lead her to ________________ herself.

26. After a woman witness has been shown to the jury to be a liar, is it better to "rub in" her guilt, or just dismiss her from the stand?

27. Under what circumstances should you not at all cross-examine a woman or a child?

28. You are on trial for feloneous assault, which allegedly occurred during a Nazi picketing demonstration in which you took part. It is charged that you struck a Jewish gentlemen and sent him to the hospital. The truth is that a huge Khazar attacked you and you had to defend yourself.

A minister who was an innocent bystander, has just testified that he witnessed you bashing the "poor fellow's" head on the sidewalk, and that you didn't stop until he was unconscious.

For all you know, this may be all the minister actually saw. You know that, although this part is true, as far as it goes, you received severe injuries yourself before gaining the upper hand in the fight.

The best thing to do is:

a) Cross-examine the minister to try to find out if he saw the Jew attack you in the first place, thereby proving self-defense;

b) Impeach the witness to try to trip him up on details, thereby throwing all of his previous testimony in a bad light;

c) Calmly say, "no questions," and pass on to another matter, saving your cross-examination for a more likely witness.

29. In the same case, a witness testifies that he saw you picketing the day he has been told a fight occurred, but he did not actually see the fight.

The best thing to do is:

a) Cross-examine to establish further that he saw you only picketing;

b) Cross-examine, asking a lot of immaterial questions, so as to make the jury think you "have something up your sleeve";

c) Say, "No questions," in such a manner as to appear as if you had just put something over on the prosecutor.

30. It is a court rule that when you are on the witness stand you must answer questions immediately when they are put to you. (True or False?)

31. It is a good idea to make a habit of answering all questions ____________ and ________________.

32. For what reason will a prosecutor ask questions of you in a rapid, machine gun-like manner, even when the questions appear to be harmless?

33. If a prosecutor bullies and harrasses you, you have every right to appeal for help from the ________________ .

34. A question with a "yes" or "no" answer is a ________ question.

35. Leading questions may be asked only in_________examination, and never may be asked in ___________ examination.

36. Cross-examination gives the defendant his only opportunity to break down the testimony of a perjured witness. (True or False?)

37. The most powerful weapon of a cross-examiner against a lying witness is _____________________ .

LESSON NO. 5
Publicity & Picketing

In setting up anti-Communist and anti-race-mixing activities in any city where the Reds and race-mixers have had their own way for years, with no opposition, you will find that your relations with the police department will go through a predictable pattern or metamorphosis.

Like everybody else in the world today (except the Communists), policemen will go to almost any lengths to avoid "trouble." In addition, policemen are charged with the duty of KEEPING THE PEACE. They are called "peace officers."

They therefore have a vested interest in preventing clashes or disturbances of all kinds within their jurisdiction. There can be no denying this.

When Communists, peace-creeps, race-mixers, and leftists have been holding unopposed demonstrations and activities in a city for years, with no reaction except talk from our side, the police get "spoiled." They come to consider such Communist, race-mixing, peace-creep, and leftist demonstrations as "normal."

AND THEREFORE THEY NATURALLY CONSIDER ANY ATTEMPT TO OPPOSE THESE CRUDS AS SOME KIND OF A "VIOLATION" OF THE STATUS QUO AND THEREFORE A MENACE TO THE PEACE THEY ARE CHARGED WITH KEEPING.

It matters not that unless SOMEBODY opposes this scum and treason, the police themselves will soon be smashed by the Reds, as they have in every country where this scum has taken over.

It has been my experience that policemen simply WILL not think that far ahead. By nature, as I have pointed out in previous lessons, policemen are on our side.

But even more THEY HATE TROUBLE!

Like millions of other Americans on our side, they prefer just to drift, politically, hoping for some sort of automatic miracle which will save them and the country from the hell-raising scum in our streets.

For all these reasons, when you first appear in the streets to make any sort of opposition at all to the enemy, you will find most police acting as though YOU were the criminal and were outraging public decency and violating the peace.

Until the "civil riots" movement got really underway just a year or so ago, the Reds and race-mixers had things to themselves and were not too rambunctious. Police had only to see that there were no acts of violence around their eternal meetings, rallies, and demonstrations. No Birchers, no "Christian Crusaders," and no other "conservatives" of any stripe whatsoever dared to appear at such Red and race-mixing affairs. Once in a while, the Klan would appear, and the police, as usual, especially in the big cities, considered this a "provocation."

Hitler writes of precisely the same phenomena among policemen in Germany when he was fighting the Communists. The Communists in Germany had become so powerful and had gained such command of the German scene, as they are now doing here, that the police considered it a "provocation" for Hitler even to announce a meeting of his own.

The Jews and Communists in New York, here in America, have been holding outright Bolshevik, Communist meetings in Union Square, New York City, for years and years. There has never been a single protest from any Jew or Jewish organization. But when I asked for a permit to speak in Union Square on behalf of the White Race and Constitution, New York went into such a tantrum as has rarely been seen even in that Red city.

You will find precisely the same situation in your city if you are just commencing operations against Communism and race-mixing. In their hearts, the police will be sympathetic to you. But when they consider their jobs, their security and the "trouble" you will cause them by opposing the enemy, their first reaction will be hostility toward you. I am sorry to have to say that they will often resort to bullying and brow-beating to try to get you to crawl back into a hole, some place, and disappear.

I am also sorry to have to report that, in many cases, although not all, policemen have discovered that they can bluff and frighten most people, especially young people on our side, with threats of jail, etc.

They expect that all they have to do is say, "Stop doing thus and so, or I'll run you in!"—and you will slink from the scene with your tail between your legs. In most cases, this has proved to be the case.

BUT THE LAW AND EVEN OUR DESPICABLE PRESENT SUPREME COURT ARE 1000% ON YOUR SIDE IF YOU INSIST ON YOUR RIGHTS TO PICKET,

DEMONSTRATE, AND SPEAK JUST AS MUCH AS THE COMMUNISTS AND RACE-MIXERS!

In spite of all the Jews and Reds in New York, I won from the U.S. Supreme Court the right to speak in Union Square, the Communist stronghold!

And in your city, YOU, TOO, CAN WIN ABSOLUTELY EQUAL RIGHTS WITH THE REDS, JEWS, AND NIGGERS!

ALL YOU HAVE TO DO IS INSIST ON YOUR RIGHTS EVEN AT THE RISK OF JAIL OR BEATINGS!

In most American cities, the first time you go forth with picket signs or literature opposing Communism and race-mixing, especially if you go as a "Nazi," the you-know-what will hit the fan and police will roust you around unmercifully.

Prepare for this. Expect it. Do not go forth unless you are spiritually fortified and ready for anything which might come before you will back down one inch on your constitutional rights.

Remember that cops who may give you a damned hard time now can become your best and closest friends later on, once they have learned to respect you as a FIGHTER!

I can truthfully say that in cities all over America, I have won the respect of police officers, judges, sheriffs, etc., who have, at first, been most unfair in their efforts to bully and frighten me because they realized that my efforts to oppose Communism and race-mixing in their cities would bring violent reactions from the enemy.

The police have some measure of reason in their natural and instant opposition to your efforts to demonstrate, distribute literature, etc.

Ninety-eight percent of such efforts by rightists, White men, and anti-Communists STINK!

I am ashamed to have to admit that almost ALL of the printed literature for distribution which dares to mention the Jewish and Negro problem which I have ever seen is printed wretchedly, is written ungrammatically and misspelled, and is worse than useless!

It actually discredits us and often hurts our cause. Certainly, it does no good whatsoever. Knowing this, many top police officers, very understandably, resent the producers of such inept and discrediting literature, picket signs, etc., completely lousing up the operation of their departments and the production of civil disorder—FOR NOTHING!

You will find that, from years of experience with knuckle-headed right-wingers and White men unable to defend their cause any way other than bashing in a nigger's head with a two-by-four, many top police officers are thoroughly disgusted with our cause, because they are disgusted with the utter incompetence and stupidity of our would-be fighters.

Even more unhappily, I must confess that police are justifiably also disgusted with the miserable COWARDICE of our would-be "fighters." Time after time, they have seen our side RUN like rabbits, the moment the possibility of loss of job or jail appears on the horizon.

I am not "attacking" my own side in telling you this. I am simply passing along professional facts you must know in order to understand and deal with police officers.

If you thoroughly understand what I have tried so hard to explain, you will not be shocked and horrified when you first step forth as a White, anti-Communist leader in public activity, and find good police officers trying their best to bully and bulldoze you out of action.

The other side of the coin is the fact that, once you have thoroughly proved to the police department that you are not some kind of a nut, that you are not incompetent or a damned fool like so many would-be "fighters" for our cause, and that you are responsible and can be depended upon, you will find the professional police officers reversing course 180° and, little by little, coming around to HELP you, whenever they can.

Whatever you do, never, never, NEVER ask any police officer for any special treatment or any favor.

No matter how much respect and liking have developed between you and the police department, always remember that policemen are professional men, that they work for pay, that they must obey orders, and that they WILL obey orders.

If they get orders to arrest you, they will arrest you.

Nine times out of ten, once they have learned to like and respect you, they will find arresting you hugely distasteful, but they will do it.

And, as a professional fighter for our side, it is your duty to BE arrested, just as much as it is the officer's duty to arrest you.

You should spare no effort, if you must be arrested by a police officer, to make the transaction as impersonal and professional as possible. Make the policeman understand that you are not shocked, horrified, or scared and that you have no personal feelings whatsoever toward him for arresting you (under all ordinary circumstances). (If some Jew or nigger cop commits an outrage upon you, of course, you should and can act appropriately. But this hardly ever happens.)

My main point in this first part of the lesson on demonstrations and anti-Communist, pro-White activities in your area is to prepare you for the inevitable phase of "persecution" you will probably experience from your local police department.

If you are not prepared to go through this, suffer the inevitable jailings and possibly beatings, and still maintain a professional attitude toward the police department, so that they will eventually respect and like you, DON'T EVEN MAKE THE FIRST MOVE!

In short, if you can't "take it," don't start it.

Before you go out on your first picket, literature distribution, or meeting-heckling operation, prepare yourself to be unfairly arrested and otherwise legally harassed by your local police department. Determine in advance that you will NEVER lose your temper, rage, act frightened, or "fight" the police department. You must steel your heart to be quietly PROFESSIONAL. You must be "cold as ice," "hard as steel," and gentlemanly of speech and deportment, no matter what outrages the police department may try in the early stages.

Remind yourself over and over that, once you have won the respect of that police department, those same policemen will actually risk their careers doing all they can, within the law, for you. They hate the Reds, niggers, Jew agitators, and treasonable beatnik scum just as much as we do. They will welcome <u>competent</u> and <u>courageous</u> allies.

<u>FIRST YOU MUST PROVE THAT YOU ARE COMPETENT AND COURAGEOUS</u>.

Now for some concrete rules on operations.

First, never picket or do anything in or near a church or synagogue.

The commies and enemy know how it affects public opinion for us to do anything in a "church," so they will hold many of their Communist meetings in Unitarian, Methodist, and nigger churches and synagogues. You can't possibly win anything by opposing this tactic. The public is simply horrified if you oppose ANYTHING in a "church"—no matter how treasonable and vicious and evil it may be and how phony is the nature of the "church"—or SYNAGOGUE.

At all other places and times, make sure your demonstration or operation of any kind is UNEQUIVOCAL.

Here, you must remember the basic principles of advertising and propaganda. People do not really care very much what you say or do. They are besieged 24 hours a day by screaming advertisements and propaganda from billboards, newspapers, television, radio, streetcar and bus advertising, signs, neon, etc., etc. They have been so beaten down and blasted by Communist and race-mixing propaganda and demonstrations that YOUR demonstration is not going to really PENETRATE their mind very deeply. You will have only a few seconds of their consciousness and almost none of their concentration in which to make your point.

SO MAKE YOUR POINT <u>SIMPLE</u>!

MAKE YOUR POINT <u>SHORT</u>!

<u>MAKE YOUR POINT SO EASY TO UNDERSTAND THAT EVEN THE STUPIDEST JERK AMONG THE PUBLIC CANNOT HELP BUT GET YOUR POINT</u>!

There are a few things that are so depressing to me as to see one of our people out picketing somewhere with a picket sign covered with small lettering from edge to edge and from top to bottom, without even a margin.

Not one person in a hundred thousand will ever read even half of such a sign. And even that one person will not be affected by the contents except to shake his head at the foolishness of the picketer.

Every picket sign should have one or two words that tell your whole story, and these words should be painted about a foot high, with the remaining words squeezed into the remaining space.

An example of what I mean here is the signs we used when the concentration camp cruds came to Washington, led by Bobby Kennedy.

Our signs looked like this:

↑Here is another example of the simplification technique.

Do not use colored cardboard for your signs. The best effect is a white poster board with black and red lettering.

It is not difficult to learn to produce first-class picket signs if you will learn one simple lettering alphabet.

Here is that alphabet. I strongly suggest that any would-be political leader learn to paint this alphabet with single strokes of a "sash brush" as we do. You can produce one of these signs in about five or ten minutes maximum with this technique, once you know how to make this alphabet.

No matter how tempting it may be, do not try to DRAW these letters as you would draw a landscape, by copying details a little at a time.

Get a big sash brush and some old newspaper, and start practicing making these letters with SINGLE STROKES of a "sash brush" and poster color.

It is of supreme importance that your picket signs look PROFESSIONAL.

When they look sloppy and amateurish, the cops will judge you to be an amateur and a "punk" and will treat you accordingly. MAKE YOUR SIGNS GOOD!

Do not use wooden sticks to hold up your picket signs. We use the cardboard tubes around which they wrap oilcloth, etc., which you can get from most dry goods stores. This will prevent charges of aggravated assault and "assault with a deadly weapon," which you will sometimes face if you have wooden picket sticks and you are attacked by Jews (and sometimes niggers).

(Your first reaction, when you see how often you will be attacked by mobs of cowardly Jews attacking in packs, and how often you are abandoned by the police, will be to want bigger and heavier picket sticks to defend yourselves.

Never forget, however, that it is better to spend a week in the hospital than ten years in prison. And five of my boys are doing prison time in San Quentin right now for wearing steel helmets and carrying heavy picket sticks to picket a Hollywood rally for Israeli bonds. Five of them were attacked by 2,000 kikes, and when they attempted to defend themselves with the picket sticks, they were charged and CONVICTED and sent to San Quentin.)

We have had several lads sent to the hospital with concussions when beaten with tire irons by Jews, etc.—BUT THEY ARE BACK IN ACTION after a session in the hospital. I know this all sounds bloody and brutal, but you would not be taking this course and studying this lesson if you were not serious about standing up to Communism and race-mixing. And if you do stand up to Communism and race-mixing in America, you must expect that you will go to jail and be beaten. But we have proved that it is not necessary to go to PRISON for LONG TERMS. Not one of my lads who have obeyed Party orders such as are written here has ever been sent up to prison for a long term. This includes me. Although I have been to jail so many times, we are considering getting up a kind of "Duncan Hines" "Guide to the Jails of America," they have never been able to convict me of anything serious or send me to prison for more than a week or so.

I realize it takes a lot of guts to step out there on the streets knowing you will face Jews with tire irons and often complete abandonment by the police who are called off by orders from Jewish-dominated mayors, etc. But I have never asked any of my boys to do anything I would not do myself, and I have survived six years, now, of this kind of action.

And I again warn and advise all students to avoid carrying wooden picket sticks or anything else which might be used to convince a jury you are carrying a weapon!

And that brings me to the next important point in this lesson.

Before you put on any kind of demonstration or action, always consider every single act, sign and situation involved in the light of how it will look to' a jury!

The Jews will never permit a trial to be held before a jury where the Jewishness of Communism or race-mixing becomes an issue in the trial. They are too damned guilty, and we would have a field day calling witnesses and proving the truth of that accusation.

On the other hand, if you are foolish enough to wear steel helmets and carry heavy picket sticks, a Jew District Attorney will have a picnic handing these frightening exhibits up and down the jury with appropriate oratory.

If you make whatever you are displaying or handing out in your demonstration sufficiently clever, so that it could not help but win the sympathy of a jury, nine times out of ten, the Jews will move heaven and earth before they will let you get in front of a jury.

That is another reason for something I have already mentioned in a previous lesson—NEVER WEAR ANYTHING "GERMAN" OR "GOOSE STEP" OR DO ANYTHING SILLY OF THIS NATURE! Jackboots, German insignia, and this sort of thing will MURDER you before an American jury. We are not Germans. Most of us are American service veterans. We admire the Germans for the stand they made for the White Race, Christianity, and anti-Communism. But any attempt to act like a bunch of "Germans" will "hang" you before a jury Don't do it!

When going out on a picket line, NEVER do anything whatsoever to "sneak."

Some of your picketers may want to wear dark glasses or otherwise disguise themselves. This is a sure way to provoke arrests and retaliation from both police and Jews.

When they think you want to play games of "hide-and-sneak," you will get the full "treatment"!

On the other hand, when you are bold as brass, and appear to be eagerly seeking "publicity" and don't care who knows your names and addresses, etc., you will find complete safety and utter silence from police, Jews, and the press. I cannot emphasize this strongly enough. For six long years now, I have seen would-be Nazis CREMATED while trying to sneak, while those who have done as I advised and been open and bold have gone on to one success after another.

In combat, I learned that the one sure way to get shot is to be constantly thinking about it and sneaking around. While you cannot be foolhardy, of course, utter boldness, combined with wisdom, kept many a man safe and alive through mortal horror. Guys like Audie Murphy and other bold men are the ones who survive and succeed. The creeps and sneaks usually get it—often right in the tail as they are trying to sneak over a coconut log, etc.

The immortal General Erwin Rommel of the Afrika Korps used to say, "Stand next to me; I'm bulletproof!"—and he was right. He WAS bulletproof.

You, too, can be "bulletproof" in demonstrations and other anti-Communist and anti-race-mixing operations by being BOLD!

Surely no one will deny that I have been as arrogant and bold in exposing and attacking Jew Communism and race-mixing as any man alive, and yet I am not in prison and I am not dead or crippled. But I know literally dozens of guys who have been sneaking around in the "Minutemen" and other such "hide-and-sneak" organizations who are in prison, have had their eyes beaten out, and are smashed for life in one way or the other.

If you must be killed or seriously hurt or go to prison for our Cause, at least do it with a "bang"—not a "whimper."

Usually, the police will insist that you identify all pickets with names and addresses. It is inconvenient, unstrategic, and sometimes irritating to have to be called aside during the picket to give this information to the police officer in charge.

We have found it is far better to arrive fully prepared with this information in written form. Following is the form we use to hand to the police officer in charge before all demonstrations and operations.

AMERICAN NAZI PARTY

928 N. Randolph St. Arl. Va. JA 4 5831

ACTIVITY RECORD

TYPE OF ACTIVITY:	DATE:
PLACE:	TIME: TO
PURPOSE:	

PARTICIPANTS

Rank	Name	Address	Age

Wording of Signs, or description of literature and other remarks:

Note the section where we list the wording on our signs. We see to it that the contents of this section (the wording of our signs) are so thoroughly truthful and therefore embarrassing to the Jews and niggers that they really hate to be forced to introduce these sheets with our names and addresses into evidence in court for the jury to read the contents of the signs.

Be sure that all members of an operation or picket, etc., have the minimum amount of money in their pockets to ensure that they cannot be charged with "vagrancy."

I cannot emphasize strongly enough that one person, AND ONLY ONE, must be in charge and, in fact, IN COMMAND!

Under present circumstances, when we are so often attacked and falsely arrested, all demonstrations and anti-Communist pro-White Christian operations require many correct and lightning-like decisions. Under "combat" conditions, menaced by Jews, niggers, and beatniks, and either threatened or abandoned by the police, you and your crew will often be scared. Do not make the mistake of pretending you are utterly "fearless." Except in the actual middle of a fight, when you are good and mad, you will be as scared and perhaps even "horrified" as I am—and the rest of us are—when confronted with some of the situations you will be forced to face trying to exert even your simplest rights in such places as Philadelphia, New York—and almost any major American city which is now almost entirely in the power of niggers, Communists, and Jews.

Under these circumstances, when pressure is put on you by the police or by outright attack, an immediate decision must be made whether to fight or retreat, whether to compromise in some way with police demands, etc., etc.

NOTHING IS MORE DEMORALIZING NOR MORE UNBECOMING THAN AN OPEN SQUABBLE AMONG YOUR GROUP ABOUT WHAT TO DO!

Under such circumstances, it is better to make an instant decision—EVEN IF IT IS WRONG—THAN TO ENGAGE IN AN UNSEEMLY SQUABBLE DURING WHICH MORALE WILL DISINTEGRATE, AND YOU WILL BECOME EASY PREY FOR BOTH POLICE AND THE ENEMY.

Before you go on such an operation, explain this carefully to all members of the group, and insist that, without exception, the group instantly obey whatever decision may be made by the leader under pressure. In the face of the enemy, display not only courage, but discipline and unity!

While on this subject, let me caution you against permitting, in your picket line, the kind of conduct which disgraces the enemy's operations.

THERE SHOULD BE NO SMOKING. THERE SHOULD BE NO SLOUCHING, NO GOSSIPING, OR ANY OTHER ACTIVITY OR LACK OF ACTIVITY WHICH DETRACTS FROM THE STERN AND SINGLE-MINDED IMAGE OF DISCIPLINE AND IRON WILL YOU MUST PROJECT.

It is far better to have a picket line of five disciplined and "sharp" men than it is to have a huge, sprawling mob of 15, 20, or 100 undisciplined, sloppy, and disorganized "rabble."

"Good motives" have nothing to do with this. You will often be approached by old folks, ladies, and others who have a sincere desire to help, and imagine that their presence on the picket line will be of help. These folks can surely help in many ways. But on a "combat" picket line, they are a tremendous millstone around your neck, and almost inevitably will insist on "privileges" and "rights" which will thoroughly disorganize your discipline and ruin your "image."

Be sure that all hands have made a "head" call before the picket and are prepared for at least three or four hours without an unseemly and rather childish demand to be excused to "wee wee."

In most circumstances, DO NOT WEAR OVERCOATS OR SWEATERS, ETC.

If you are picketing in uniform, wear whatever warm clothing you can, UNDERNEATH your uniform.

You would be surprised at the grudging respect you will win from police and even the enemy when you stay out there on a picket line with steely determination in freezing, bitter, and even stormy weather without running for cover, as the enemy always does.

If one of the members of your picket group is attacked by the enemy, as often happens, you have two courses of conduct.

First, if the police are right on the job and present in sufficient numbers, the other members of the picket group and the leader should step back and permit the police to handle the incident. ANY OTHER CONDUCT WILL THOROUGHLY INCENSE THE POLICE THEMSELVES AND INVOLVE ALL OF YOU IN PERHAPS SERIOUS CHARGES. Thus, the police will quickly stop the violence and will usually apprehend both participants. Then the matter can be settled in court.

On the other hand, when we are purposefully abandoned by the police, as we often are when they pointedly disappear one or two blocks from the scene and hide around corners, etc., with orders to permit us to be attacked, it is the duty of all present to give all possible assistance to whoever is attacked.

But remember the rule of law that you have no "right" of "self-defense"—to use any more force than is necessary to stop the violence and protect life and limb. Once you have reached the point where you are physically masters of the situation, any "beating" of the attacker will be legally considered assault and possibly "aggravated assault", etc.

The temptation to beat the living hell out of these filthy attackers, who never cease to howl and moan about "freedom" for Communists and other scum to picket, but who attack us physically at every opportunity, will be overwhelming. But do not give in to this temptation. Simply hold the attacker and holler for the police to pick him up.

IF AT ALL POSSIBLE, TRY TO HAVE A PHOTOGRAPHER, PREFERABLY WITH A MOTION PICTURE CAMERA SECRETED WHERE HE CAN RECORD ANY SUCH INCIDENTS.

Remember to detach such a photographer from the group and do not speak to him where the enemy can see, since, if they realize he is with you, they will also attack him AND HIS CAMERA.

We have found it effective to locate a window on the second story somewhere near the picket scene where the cameraman can have a good and close view of the scene. Alternatively, the cameraman can pose as a "newsman" and then make himself scarce—with his precious film—after any such incident.

More than once, we have wrecked Jewish "frames" by showing such films in court.

Be careful of picketing near tough bars.

It is easy for Jews to go into a bar and inflame a lynch mob to come out and attack you (while the Jews remain safely inside the bar, rubbing their hands).

If you must picket near a crowded, working-class bar, be thoroughly aware of this danger and, if possible, station one of your non-combatant types in the bar as a witness and intelligence agent. This is where older people—and sometimes even women—can be of great help.

Nothing is more important in the success of a picket or other such operation than the ISSUE you choose to attack.

Always try to conduct your operations against the MOST UNPOPULAR issue being pushed by the enemy.

Thus, do not picket Jews, per se, in the South, unless there is no choice. Too few people in the Deep South yet understand the Jewish problem.

But they sure as hell understand the nigger problem, and a picket against a bunch of filthy, Communist race-mixers will be highly popular, given that you are in a Nazi uniform.

I do not mention this because we are cowardly or afraid to fight unpopular issues.

Usually, you will be too hard-pressed and will have too few people and resources to picket on all issues. So why throw your resources and people away in a battle in which you are at least half licked before you start?

Further, at least in the early stages of your operations in a new city, you will almost always wind up in court. And it is mighty comforting to go before a jury with an issue in which the jury will be 100% on your side rather than the other way around. It also breeds success and survival.

Do not permit your pickets to TALK—especially do not permit them to respond to provocations by the enemy!

You are not out there to argue and dispute. You are out there to DEMONSTRATE! The Jews, especially, will often try to provoke your pickets, etc., into altercations in which they can appear the "innocent victims." If you or any of your group succumb to this tremendous temptation, you will be playing directly into their hands and quite possibly setting yourself up for some jail or prison time.

One of the most horrendous examples of this sort of thing, which will take guts for you even to read, is the business of Jew-spitting. These Jewish liars and hypocrites who pretend to love free speech (for Communists) so dearly are great "spitters."

In the early days of your operations in a new city, when the police are still highly hostile, and where you will be too weak to maintain any sort of sustained court battle, the kikes usually come out in platoons and brigades TO SPIT ON YOU.

REMEMBER THAT THE OBJECT OF EVERYTHING YOU DO IS TO SUCCEED—TO WIN!

Your personal satisfaction or feeling of "revenge," etc., has nothing whatsoever to do with it. Remember, I warned at the beginning not to start operations unless you can really "take it."

And the hardest thing in the world to take is a big glob of Jew spit on your face. Your natural, God-given instinct will be to knock down the filthy Jew who does such a thing. But remember, his purpose is to cause you to do precisely that, so that he can then see you packed off to prison.

I am sorry to have to report that I have had Jews actually spit in my face in front of a police officer, with the police officer doing absolutely nothing, as the Jew knew in advance. The Jew, usually a little guy, then goads you to distraction, trying to get you to hit him. And the policeman is standing there, usually under orders from political prostitutes somewhere, waiting for you to give him the excuse to grab you for "aggravated assault," etc.

If you cannot control your natural instincts and go for this "bit," you are GONE.

It matters not that you were spit upon and that any decent citizen has the absolute right to give a good beating to any person who spits on him. In the early stages, when political prostitutes will be able to control the police, the police will usually never even "see" the spit.

Once, I went to a high police officer right after such an incident and showed him the glob of Jew spit trickling down my face and pointed out the Jew who had done it. The cop, obviously uncomfortable, told me, "I don't see no spit!"

He "won't see it" in court either. Thus, you will be made to appear as a bully who simply physically attacked a Jew smaller than you and beat him unmercifully. (You will be amazed and forced to accord grudging admiration to these Jew actors when you see how they can limp and appear crippled for life after a glancing blow or a slight shove.)

The best and only real defense against these spitters is a motion picture camera.

But even then, in cities like Philadelphia and in most other cities in the early stages of your operation, you will simply have to steel yourself to be spat upon and to be helpless for a while.

After one of these spitting sessions where I was hit at least three times by these cowardly Jew swine, I went to the U.S. Attorney and tried to swear out a warrant against the Jews who did it--when I had WITNESSES. The U.S. Attorney simply told me it was no crime to spit on people, and he could not issue the warrant. I thereupon informed him that I planned to go down to the B'nai B'rith building the next day and wait until the Jews came out after work, when our group would line up on both sides of the sidewalk and spit on all the Jews to our hearts content, since it was not a crime.

He thereupon cynically and brutally informed me that any such action would result in our immediate arrest under every charge in the book.

Do not gasp and protest that this is an outrage, "unjust," etc. It is simply a fact you will have to deal with and be prepared for.

When you know for sure that you will face illegal police harassment, threats, and bullying, or when it is supremely important, legally, to have verbal permission from some official to do a certain thing, you should never approach such an official or the police without a small portable tape recorder in your pocket connected to a lapel microphone. Carefully record all key conversations with police officers and other officials involved. It is also a good idea to record any altercations with attackers, etc.

If you have carefully done this, and then you are arrested, try to get the whole tape recorder and tape in the hands of a justice or magistrate as soon as possible, along with an explanation of what it is, so that you cannot later be charged with having tampered with the tape.

One of the key elements of a good picket is POSITION.

When you are counter-picketing, which will be at least half the time, try to preempt the best position by getting there very early. Nobody has the right to "reserve" any area for picketing unless they have some sort of permit, which is usually not required in most cities. Nor do the police have the right to move you to give a choice spot to the niggers, Jews, and Communists—although they almost always attempt to do this at the behest of rotten politicians at the top.

In most cases, this is one instance in which I strongly recommend courteous but absolutely firm resistance to police orders to move. Police have the absolute right to move you along whenever they must do so to preserve the peace, and it is impossible for them to maintain order otherwise because they are being overwhelmed.

If they have men and resources to do so, it is their absolute duty to accord you your rights by holding off mobs, etc. But if they are being overwhelmed, they also have the right to demand that you cease and desist, and you should obey.

But if they simply order you to move around the corner into obscurity so that some Jews, niggers, beatniks, and Reds can have a choice picketing spot, you should simply refuse even at the cost or risk of arrest or abuse. Just make sure you are on solid ground, and that there is no mob present, and that you can prove in court the police were simply trying to give the best picketing spot to late comers—Jews, niggers, beatniks, etc., with no justification whatsoever. You will win in court as we always have in these cases.

On the other hand, always try your best to cooperate with decent cops.

Many times, you will find that your operations will cause them to work extra shifts, etc. If they are halfway decent, and they ask you to quit a little bit early to prevent them from being forced to put on still another shift, etc., I recommend you bend over backward to cooperate.

Remember that the sooner you can win the respect of the police and make them LIKE you, the sooner your operations will become relatively safe and easy, and the sooner you will have the commies. Jews, niggers, and beatnik scum whipped. It is worth "backing up" quite a bit to win the respect and liking of your police department.

It goes without saying that you should never compromise on a matter of principle or right with police officers, especially when they are trying to "push" or bully you.

But when they ask you, as a favor, and, with good cause, to modify your plans a bit, and this will not compromise your rights or principles, by all means go along.

I will close this lesson with a word about purpose.

Remember that, even if 10,000 people personally see your picket line, this is "peanuts" compared to the results you will get if you succeed in winning major press, radio, and TV coverage, etc.

(The Jews know this, of course, and the lengths to which they will go to censor us from the news, while giving major coverage to commies, etc., are unbelievable!)

Nevertheless, with really clever tactics and dogged determination, you can often FORCE the news media to cover your operations.

One way of doing this is to make sure that, while legal, your operations are so "controversial " and arrogantly obvious that so many people will see and know that if the Jews DON'T cover your operations, they will be forced to expose the degree of their censorship of the news media.

Therefore, again, make your signs SIMPLE and easily readable from across the street, so that they can be read on TV, etc. One sign shown on TV for two seconds is worth a picket line a hundred men strong for two whole days.

But if your picket signs are equivocal or hard to read or contain too many words, all the TV in the world will be wasted on you.

To sum up, therefore, pick the right issue, stab at the heart of it with powerful slogans and a few key words painted as large as possible, and maintain absolute discipline and order on your picket line.

Persistence, courage, and wise choice of issues and slogans are the key to success in these demonstrations.

Don't start if you aren't ready to finish—all the way. Then get out there and stick with it!

The enemy consists of liars, cheats, cowards, and finks of the worst sort.

We have the truth on our side. If we back it with quiet, competent, and utterly courageous determination, we <u>can't</u> lose.

LESSON NO. 5
Test Questions

1. Policemen are always hostile to anti-Communists and pro-White demonstrators. (True or false)

2. Relations with the police department in your city will usually change. (True or false)

3. Because of their very nature, policemen tend to be rightists. (True or false)

4. Policemen have the absolute right, under any circumstances, to stop any demonstration in order to fulfill their duty of keeping the peace. (True or false)

5. What is the best way to change the attitude of the police department toward the rightwing, anti-Communist, and pro-White demonstrations?

6. Give three reasons why police in any city where we have just begun to operate will usually be hostile.

7. There is no use in carrying our cases to the pro-Red Supreme Court. (True or false)

8. You should always obey orders by police officers to "move along." (True or false)

9. It is a good practice, to protect the identity of members of a picketing group, to have them wear dark glasses and make every effort to disguise themselves. (True or false)

10. When Communists are holding a meeting in a synagogue, you should picket with signs emphasizing that the Communists are using "religion" as a disguise. (True or false)

11. What is the main purpose and value in a picket line?

12. The reason it is important to put as much information as possible on each picket sign is that the public has no other way of getting the suppressed facts. (True or false)

13. One of the main reasons police in your city will, at first, be hostile and interfere with your demonstrations is because they hate ____________________.

14. What is the best answer if you are picketing and a Jew calls you a "son-of-a-bitch" or a "M- F-"?

15. How should you act if arrested by friendly police?

16. Describe the special circumstances under which you may request special treatment or small favors from the police department.

17. Explain why picket signs should be as short and punchy as possible.

18. On a separate sheet of paper, with single strokes of your pencil, draw the alphabet recommended for picket signs.

19. On the opposite side of the same sheet of paper, draw a miniature reproduction of the sign you would use to picket Martin Luther Coon if he came to your town trying to force the "bussing" of White students to nigger schools.

20. If a picket of ours is attacked, all of our Nazis always attack the attacker with ferocity and honor to teach that Jews better not try the same thing again. (True of false)

21. Describe the best kind of picket sticks to use and give your reasons.

22. What future possible event should you always think about in considering every demonstration, action, act, sign, or situation in which you will be involved?

23. What articles of uniform and what actions must you absolutely forbid all of your pickets to wear and/or do?

24. Why?

25. What is the single most important factor in setting up the administration of a picket line?

26. Describe all the steps in conducting a good picket operation from beginning to end.

27. What is the best kind of issue to use in picketing?

28. How can a political group "reserve" a good area in which to picket?

29. Name the MAJOR tactical objective in any picket line.

30. What should you do if a police officer in charge of the squad covering your operations asks you to quit 15 minutes early so he can save an entire new squad from coming on duty overtime?

31. What is your one possibility of FORCING the Jew censors to report your demonstrations and activity in spite

of the usual “blackout”?

LESSON NO. 6
Legal Attacks On The Enemy

Much of the instructions in this lesson I learned from the Jews, who taught me the hard way, by performing the experiments on me.

We, of course, can never get away with the raw deals pulled by the Jews, who are always exonerated in court when they start the usual moaning about the gas chambers, and how their whole family was gassed, usually several times apiece.

But the Jews have taught me one invaluable lesson: how to avoid group liability for the acts of members.

Our demonstrations have been attacked a hundred times by wild heebs, often in military formation. But when they arrive in court, the sweet, lovable kikes moan about how they were "carried away" by seeing our demonstration, and they know the other Jews are all ashamed of them, etc., etc.—and their act was simply on the spur of the moment. The courts almost always "oh" and "ah" over this heart-rending explanation sobbed out by the Jews, and they come right back next day and do it again, by platoons, regiments, and brigades.

This has taught me that we Nazis must never do naughty things like busting up Communist meetings, etc.

Of course, once in a while, some of our members get carried away entirely by the treason going on and bust up Commie meetings regardless of this firm policy of command headquarters. I, of course, deplore the unfortunate conduct of the stormtroopers who thus disrupted the nice Red meeting, but explain that they were simply unable to restrain themselves when they were confronted by naked treason to the United States.

All students are cautioned, therefore, NOT to break up Commie meetings. It is wrong and very, very naughty.

However, I will explain some of the methods some of our lads have found very effective when they were overcome with what we call "National Socialist Involuntary Reactions," or NSIR.

First comes the matter of WHICH meetings to work on.

Only the most FLAGRANT, RED meetings and demonstrations call for the NSIR. Any strong tactics on pantywaist liberal outfits backfire because a lot of the saps attending are sincere, and rough stuff just convinces them of the rightness of their leadership. It is also deadly dangerous to get mixed up with such tactics against any meeting which is not obviously RED to the general public. It makes US look like the "bullies" the Reds claim we are. But when you go after the Fair Play For Cuba Committee, for instance, the public (and a jury) will be pretty much with you so long as you stay away from murder, arson, and such things. Hornets, shouters, red paint, eggs, platform jumpers, etc., will be enjoyed by most of the public in such cases.

If the meeting or operation to be "treated" is REALLY Red, such as the Vietnam Reds who are jumping on U.S. troop trains and thereby committing sedition against the U.S.A., I personally and officially recommend, not harassment, but citizens' ARREST. As a citizen, you have the right and the duty to seize, detain, and deliver to the proper authorities any person who commits a FELONY in your presence. And stopping a troop train is sedition, a number one felony. But you must have the written law in your hands at the time; you must be SURE of what you are doing, and you must be prepared to face all kinds of charges and civil proceedings, from kidnapping to false arrest. In the case of the bastards stopping U.S. troop trains, I personally don't care what they hit me with; I intend to grab the first filthy Red who tries to stop a U.S. troop train while American boys are dying over there in Vietnam.

But when the Reds are not quite so open about it and are holding a meeting to advocate and preach treason, there is a graduated list of things you can do to "express your own opinion" of the ideological garbage being flung around, under our free speech laws.

Here, the Reds have thoughtfully provided us with a thousand charming precedents.

Over the years, there has been almost no OPEN opposition to Communist hell-raising. They do as they damned well please, and they don't tolerate anti-Communist meetings. When I first began to hold anti-Communist rallies out in the open, the Yids arrived to break them up by FORCE, by SCREAMING, and other sweet, reasonable, Jewish-type methods.

The more desperate the kikes became to stop me, and the more raw their methods got, the more the courts had to twist and squeeze things to rule that their vile, organized howling and screaming, their heaving of garbage at us, and their physical attacks were "free speech" under the Bill of Rights.

But now these precedents have been set for all time. And

what is legal for Jews must be legal for US.

So we use these same decisions when the Hebrews come on with Gus Hall & Co.

If they can organize howling choruses of three and four hundred Jews to scream on signal to drown US out, then we can organize a chorus to drown out the Jews—and we do. So can you. It's just called "heckling." All you do is find a flock of people who all feel the same urge at the same time to SCREAM their opposition to a speaker, and he is silenced. In fact, if there is enough hubbub, the police usually claim there is the certainty of some sort of riot, and SHUT UP THE SPEAKER. This has usually been ME—but it can also be Gus Hall or any other Red who tries to speak. There is a special trick in this "free speech" screaming. The whole group must "feel the urge to scream SIMULTANEOUSLY— whenever the speaker opens his mouth. After fifteen or twenty minutes of this, the hardiest speaker will fold up and surrender.

There is also the business of motorcycles and trucks. I have often discovered that wherever I have set up to speak, there will be some Jew having starting difficulty with his motorcycle or truck, and he finds it necessary to rev it up considerably to be sure it is going. Now that we have learned that this is-his sacred "right," we have experienced the same kind of difficulties near Jew-Communist meetings, often having additional problems with backfiring.

At inside meetings, we have also suffered from Jews expressing their "free speech" by placing various unpleasant substances in the air conditioner ducts. A rotten clam strategically placed will discourage most meetings. And a clam gets pretty rotten if kept warm and cozy for a week or so.

A bag-full of aggravated hornets or yellow-jackets is also handy in certain situations.

A more gentle method of accomplishing surprising results is mice. A few dozen little, crawly, furry white mice let loose on the darkened floor of an auditorium full of liberal, nigger-loving ladies, during a film showing will do wonders for your free speech, although we never do things like this, and you shouldn't either.

Perhaps the best methods, however, are those which make damned fools out of the enemy.

During the NAACP convention here in Washington, my boys were plagued with NSIR's every day of the convention. Somebody sneaked into the lobby where the welcoming committee was handing out the programs and directory sheets to the incoming niggers, swiped a sample sheet, changed all the times and room numbers, and replaced the regular pile with the "revised" edition, printed in a matter of hours. Niggers were bursting into the wrong rooms for a full week, showing up at the wrong times for the wrong committee meetings, and roundly cursing their arrangements committee for their foul-ups.

During the main banquet, one of our officers, wearing blackface, managed to leap onto the head table and rush up and down it between the olives, ashtrays, and water glasses, throwing boat tickets left and right and hollering, "Ah's your Uncle Remus come to take you niggers back home to Africa!" Four other nigger meetings were treated to similar visits by Nazi "Niggers" with boat tickets, etc. At the height of one nigger meeting, dozens of mice were dropped from a balcony on the assembled coons.

Several of us have managed to get on the mailing lists of most of the Red and race-mixing organizations, and these outfits have been suffering from phony invitations. Somehow, every time we get invited to some quiet little Red or race-mixing meeting in some Heebs home, hundreds of niggers and other people get similar invitations and show up to make a total mess of the affair. I certainly hope none of our lads are mixed up in this sort of nasty trick, as I, of course, cannot approve of any such things.

During the course of their National Socialist Involuntary Reactions, even while they are "carried away" with the heat of the thing, many of my boys find themselves scheming and planning just as if they were quite reasonable and clear-thinking. In this phase, I am told, some of them who are experiencing NSIRs simultaneously get together and actually coordinate their involuntary reactions.

One of the most amazing things about this rational phase of the NSIR is the way my lads have organized diversionary demonstrations. It's the oldest trick in the book, but it always works.

Whenever it is necessary to get one man into a ticklish spot for an operation, some of the other lads find themselves completely carried away with an NSIR in the other direction. While the Jews or niggers or whatever are all scrambling toward the disturbance in one place, the key man has been able to move in quietly for the main event.

Disguise, or "costume" fun, is indispensable for this sort of operation.

Nobody ever worries about waiters at a banquet, and it is not illegal to wear the same kind of clothes as a waiter, with a towel over the arm. Quite a few "waiters" have turned out to be Nazis having NSIR fits right in the middle of nigger cotillions or banquets, etc. The same goes for bell boys, messenger boys, etc.

It is absolutely UNBELIEVABLE what one can get away with, with naked NERVE.

One of my lads just knocks on the door of the big scene, and when it is opened a crack, says he has the "script" for Mr. so-and-so, then tiptoes ever so quietly up to the head table with the help of the doorkeepers, etc., until he is ready to start shouting and raging in the middle of Mr. so- and-so's speech.

When they are expecting you, that's the time for the

"dummy" attack. Several well-known members of the organization should make a clumsy job of "sneaking" into position, while a new man or a disguised member gets set for the real "free speech." While the committee members are surrounding and dealing with the suspected disrupters, the real one is in a perfect position for a real surprise. I myself often feel the urge to attend such meetings, and since I am quite well known, things are in such an uproar wherever I am that some of the other lads can achieve their purpose with no interference.

Another highly successful, but more painful, operation is straight, platform-grabbing. Here, the man suffering from the NSIR simply strides quickly up to the platform, moves in on the microphone or podium, and SPEAKS. In many cases, the dumbfounded liberals and Reds will simply stagger back aghast. Other Nazis in the audience shout, "Let him speak! Let him speak!"

If the regular speaker is breaking the law with pornography or treason, etc., it is also possible simply to shove this criminal to one side and announce the meeting closed, put the offender under citizens' arrest, and start hollering for the cops.

Then there is the "special-action" operation, calling for imagination.

Take the case of the organized queers of America, who held a convention right here in Washington, at the Sheraton Park Hotel. I felt that a picket would be beneath our dignity. Queers are too vile to fight or picket. And literature would not do the job either. What was called for was something which would dramatize the REVOLTING nature of these creeps and their damnable "convention." So I had a big grocery box all wrapped up in pretty pink paper with ribbons all over it, and huge signs lettered all over it, "24 QUARTS OF VASELINE. RUSH! TO QUEER CONVENTION, Sheraton Park Hotel, c/o Rabbi in charge." Robert Lloyd, carrying the pink box, then burst into the swanky lobby of the best hotel in Washington, where the fairies were convening, shouting, "Here's the Vaseline, where are the queers?" He was able to get all the way through the lobby with the pink package of "Vaseline" and all the way into the queer meeting. The faggots began to go ape, screaming and crying and moaning; one even paid him $5 to leave. When the police arrived, they laughed so hard they couldn't arrest him for a few minutes, and the queers became downright hysterical.

The most potent weapon to use in calling public attention to the evil activities of Communists and other disloyal agitators is <u>HUMOR</u>!

When a bunch of African cannibals posing as diplomats and dignitaries from the phony African nation of "Upper Volta" were being given the VIP treatment by Washington officials, with limousine parades down Pennsylvania Avenue, etc., I decked out a group of our men in blackface with sultan robes and turbans, feathers and other bigger favorite costumes, and put them in a pickup truck labeled "We is de delegates from LOWER Volta" lettered on the side, and one of our "niggers" was wielding a mop over the head of "de King," in the finest traditions of African potentates. We followed the "Upper Volta" niggers and their limousines around with our "Lower Volta" niggers and signs such as "Us demands more foreign aid and more tender missionaries"—to the huge delight of the populace—and the immense discomfiture of the nigger "dignitaries" and their black fanny-kissing State Department escorts.

When peace-creeps come to Washington for vigils and burning themselves on behalf of peace, etc., we appear with buckets of gasoline and thatches and signs reading "Free gasoline and matches, courtesy American Nazi Party."

On the first day of school in Dallas, Texas, as the niggers were being rammed into more schools, our Dallas unit arrived with a chimpanzee and demanded that it be enrolled along with the niggers. (The school authorities, long intimidated and conditioned by nigger arrogance, meekly supplied the proper forms, and our monkey attended school for a whole day!)

Laughter-provoking heckling during an enemy speech is always legal, of course, and can be deadly. To be effective, this sort of heckling must not be merely insulting, but must be both the barbed truth and funny. I have found by experience that if the shout is funny enough, it will get a whole audience, even hostile to you, laughing at one of their own friends, much to his misery.

One of the problems you will run into in dealing with enemy meetings of Communists, etc., is getting our man or men back out of the Red mob alive.

For this need, we have developed a technique which, in my opinion, is worth the full price you paid for this course.

Before I reveal this almost miraculous technique for surviving Communist, Jew, and nigger meetings, let me once again warn the student that it is not only illegal to impersonate a police officer or usurp police powers, but it is guaranteed to bring down the wrath of even a sympathetic police department upon you.

However, so long as you do not in any way indicate or imply that you are police or acting as police, it is perfectly legal to do all in your power to prevent violence and maintain order at any meeting in your presence.

Therefore, after one of our men has suffered a National Socialist Involuntary Reaction and made a speech from an enemy platform, we have found that the following technique will almost always help maintain order, prevent violence—<u>and get our man safely out of the hall</u>.

Two heavy-set, well-dressed, and clean-cut men from our group hauled the Nazi speaker off the platform very brusquely, pinned both of his arms behind his back, and marched him out of the hall—a "prisoner."

As the "prisoner" is being taken out, his captors are ordering the crowd to "stand aside," "he's in our custody," or "clear the way," etc. These words uttered by the "captors" are of such psychological impact that the crowd quickly obeys without the slightest objection.

The assembled Communist Jews, Shabaz-Goy or niggers will almost always PRESUME that the Nazi is under arrest and on the way to jail.

Once outside, of course, the "prisoner" is soundly congratulated and clapped on the back by his two "captors," while the enemy rages impotently.

I repeat, in using this method, you must be EXTREMELY careful not to interfere with or in any way imitate police officers. The fact that two of our men look like detectives to somebody else, with no effort on their part, is no violation of any law whatsoever, and the two men are actually and in truth preventing disorder and possible violence. But if police officers are in the area and in any way make any move, it is our duty to cooperate 100% with the police officers.

Even if it is only the Communist Jews, etc., who challenge the two "escorts," if they are asked, "Are you policemen?" they must, of course, answer "No." Nor may our "escorts" lay hands on or in any way interfere with the scum at the meeting—unless they are attacked.

It goes without saying that in all such operations, all participants must be scrupulously careful not only not to be armed, but not to have on their persons any item which could even be *considered* a weapon—not even a pocket knife.

A method I have heard of, but certainly cannot recommend because of several considerations, is the advance re-wiring of the enemy public address system. It is my understanding that some unscrupulous types have had the electronic knowledge, the boldness, and the cleverness to sneak into the area of an enemy meeting, install a cut-in switch to the P.A. system, and arrange for a speech over the loud speakers on the subject of "back to Africa" or "the gas chamber for Communist Jew traitors" in the middle of the enemy meeting.

The Jews have taught me another method of "meeting busting"—which I cannot recommend, of course, since it is, I believe, illegal. What they have done is to have vast numbers of delivery men all arrive at the scene with dozens of orders of fried chicken, flowers, collect telegrams, etc.—all *C.O.D.*!

Another example of platform-grabbing took place during the campaign for Governor here in Virginia. Capt. John Patler, for some strange reason, put on his best suit of clothes, pinned a large Republican campaign button to his lapel, and went off to attend a "Holton (Republican candidate) for Governor" rally in a local high school auditorium.

Patler sat up as close to the stage as he could get. After the preliminary speakers, candidate Holton made a grand entrance into the auditorium from the rear with much fanfare. Everyone in the audience went wild with applause. So did Capt. Patler, for some inexplicable reason. Holton headed down the aisle, waving to his supporters and shaking hands on his way to the stage. Capt. Patler stood up and shook hands with Holton, each smiling into the other's face!

As Holton began his speech, some inconsiderate person in the rear of the hall turned on a portable radio full blast with loud, vile, nigger music. Some of Holton's goons rushed to the rear of the auditorium. The man who had the radio in his possession stood up and *loudly* apologized. "I can't turn it off! It's stuck, I'm sorry!" shouted the man with the radio, as he *slowly* went out the rear door. The entire audience, including the speaker and those on stage with him, all focused their attention on the disruption. At that precise moment, while the opposition was distracted, Capt. Patler ran from his seat at the front of the audience, leaped onto the stage, and had a "National Socialist Involuntary Reaction." He ripped a Holton campaign poster off the speaker's podium, leaving part of it hanging. He lunged for the microphone. Holton retreated. The Nazi shouted, "Holton is selling out the White people of Virginia!" Before he could do or say much, Patler was thrown off the stage headfirst into the waiting arms of a bunch of goons who had rushed up to the stage to grab him.

By now, the whole audience was in an uproar. Suddenly, more than a dozen young men in different parts of the audience began shouting, "Let him speak! Let him speak! Don't hurt him!" Some of the audience picked up the chant. Afterward, we discovered to our amazement that the dozen or so young men were actually Nazis who just happened to attend the Holton rally as individuals. Each of them had simultaneously decided to pin on a Republican campaign button and attend the rally. Each of them behaved as enthusiastically as one would expect a Republican supporter to be at a Republican rally.

As the Nazi on stage fell into the hands of the goons who were about to tear him apart, two well dressed, clean-cut, older-looking men in trench coats pushed their way over to Patler, each grabbed one of his arms and announced "he's in our custody ... clear a path ... he's in our custody," as they pulled their "prisoner" up through the aisle and out the building where they shoved him into a car, released him and, shook his hand. (It seems the two gentlemen turned out to be two Nazis who, through sheer coincidence, also just happened to attend the Holton rally that night.)

We later discovered that, during the confusion, some devilish fiend also released a dozen White mice in the audience, and several eggs were hurled at the speaker's platform.

The meeting was eventually restored to order. But the crowd was never at ease again as their eyes focused on the torn campaign poster on the podium, which served as a constant reminder of the slogan shouted by Patler.

On certain occasions, *prolonged* disruption is caused by

individuals in different sections of the audience jumping from their seats at different intervals of a meeting, so that the Red speaker is faced with continual disruption throughout the entire speech.

Literature should be distributed on parked autos in the area surrounding the meeting hall. Door handles are ideal spots for placing literature. This way, the literature goes unnoticed until the car is entered by its owner. Literature on windshields attracts attention, and the opposition may take them off the cars.

Once you have become fairly well known, a very effective method of penetrating enemy meetings is to let it be known in advance that you are going to picket OUTSIDE the meeting. When I have done this, the enemy troops usually wait outside to pounce on me when we appear. I then send a few diversionary troops to picket outside. Often, the enemy speakers cannot get their troops back inside the auditorium to start the meeting because they are all outside waiting for me.

Meanwhile, Party members stealthily dressed and bearded as beatniks, peace creeps, and other assorted traitors, can infiltrate the meeting and place themselves strategically in the hall.

It is, of course, impossible for a man seized with a fit of coughing to help himself until the seizure has passed. You would be surprised what these coughing fits can do to an enemy meeting if they take place from different parts of the hall one after the other, every time the enemy speaker is ready to start again.

I will close this lesson with a lesson taught to me by the crafty Jews—for your guidance and possible use.

When we have succeeded in picketing or demonstrating against some Jewish outrage in front of some Jewish organization, we have often caught the heebs preparing their FEMALE demonstration buster around a corner—WITH A PEELED ONION! Once the tears are flowing freely, the Jewish "lady" comes shrieking around the corner, tearing and clawing with her fingernails at our demonstrators and our signs, screaming about how her folks were gassed two or three times in concentration camps, etc., etc., etc.

No matter what these Jewish hellions do in the way of violence and assault, they have always been exonerated and highly praised in court by the judge who practically sobs out his deep sympathy as the vicious Jewess sits up there demurely and modestly with her eyes lowered and squeezing the onion at her eyes to keep the tears flowing smoothly.

Remembering this fact, a young lady (member of the Party) once rushed up onto the platform where a convicted Communist, Frank Wilkinson, was speaking at American University, and she gave him the female tigress act, claws and all. It worked! There was no serious prosecution, and you may be sure that THAT Communist meeting was a total mess.

To sum up, the secret of successfully busting up meetings of traitors to our Constitution is a sort of legal "brinkmanship." We are not criminals and lawbreakers. The enemy is all of these things. The enemy has regularly attacked us by assault and violence and broken up our meetings, and we use these precedents for what they call their "free speech" to smite them with the other edge of their own sword.

In countering their treason, you should make every possible effort to reduce the possibilities of mob violence and civil disorder and to cooperate to the maximum possible extent with your local police. Using the methods recommended in this lesson, you will find that you can be a very terrible scourge to Communist traitors-and race-mixers in your area any time they try to hold one of their treason orgies—without having you or your members do any "big time" on serious charges. If you are dead serious, as we are, about fighting treason, you will be proud and happy to serve the 10 to 30 day sentences you will probably draw for disorderly conduct, even though the enemy is often praised in our courts for doing precisely what you will be doing.

I will leave you with this thought to keep when and if you wind up sitting in a cell—usually surrounded by niggers. The path to the palace ALWAYS lies through its dungeons.

The men who have really achieved on both sides of this final battle of Armageddon between Communism and the White Race have ALWAYS been sent to the jails and prisons, usually many times.

If you don't go to jail fighting for a White, Christian, Constitutional America, you're not going any place in the movement at all. The Jews crucified Christ and, you may depend on it, they will most assuredly throw you in their dungeons—at the very least—if you expose and/or oppose them.

And now, go to it—AND GOOD LUCK!

LESSON NO. 6

Test Questions

1. What does the enemy try to "stick us" with whenever one of our men heroically attacks a communist meeting or demonstration?

2. How should a leader be sure the Jews cannot succeed in this?

3. Why is this method legal?

4. What sort of meetings are the only ones which should be considered for "protest," and WHY?

5. What can you do if the enemy is openly breaking the law as in draft-card burning or treasonable stopping of U.S. troop trains?

6. What is the secret of the mass VOCAL protest?

7. Name at least one good method of demonstrating a powerful protest against a commie outdoor meeting in the streets.

8. What is the most deadly weapon in the arsenal of protest outside of violence itself?

9. Name some methods of getting a man into an important position without being observed, even though the position is in public view?

10. What can you do when the enemy is conducting such a VILE affair or demonstration that he is beneath the notice of an honorable picket or platform scramble?

11. How can you get a protester out of the enemy hall safely and without getting arrested?

12. What must you be especially careful of in doing this?

13. Before the leader of an "invasion" group stakes off for the operation, what should he be sure his lads do NOT have with them? WHY?

14. What kind of special action protester is especially effective and how should this type of action be used?

15. Is it possible to conduct good operations against communist meetings and still remain on good terms with the police? Explain.

16. What should all meeting-protesters understand before they are allowed to proceed?

17. What can you do in the middle of a communist meeting which is absolutely legal and yet will stop the treasonable meeting? Describe how it could be done.

18. Name one very vulnerable piece of equipment in an enemy rally or speech and what might be done with it.

19. What is one of the best methods of getting into banquets and dinner meetings, outside of buying a ticket?

20. What is the best way to keep informed of enemy activity in your area?

LESSON NO. 7
Leadership No. 1

No problem will cause a would-be White leader as much pure, unadulterated MISERY and heartbreak as trying to deal with the kind of individualistic, courageous, ornery, and just plain cussed men who are willing to stand shoulder-to-shoulder with us in the last and greatest struggle of our race to survive.

No "normal" person, by the very definition of the word "normal," will ever be attracted to such a rabid, counter-revolutionary movement such as ours, which requires the recruit to give his all and receive almost nothing in return except ideological satisfaction and pride in his heroic leadership of his race.

"Normal," by definition, means that which is average.

And no "average" person, in a million years, ever made a revolution or provided the leadership to stop one, as we are now doing.

Thus, it is clear that while our movement is so small, persecuted, and relatively immature, we must not only expect, but we must be temporarily satisfied with many fellow fighters for our cause who would never be tolerated in any business, social, or other ordinary organization.

Men and women seek out and find the American Nazi Party and are willing to suffer much to join and fight with us, not because they are conformists, but specifically because they are NON-conformists who absolutely refuse to bend their necks to Jewish, nigger, and Communist tyranny as most of the rest of Americans bend their necks for the creeps now dominating America. Our kind of people are the hardest sort of men and women in the world to organize and discipline, precisely because they have already rebelled from the discipline and organization attempted to be imposed on them by the Jews. They are natural-born rebels, revolutionaries—and thus, potentially—MUTINEERS.

They have a low tolerance point for any form of coercion or enforced discipline.

Now, starting with that material, add the fact that in any organization you may lead, you will have neither reward nor punishment in the usual sense to apply as "pries" to your "troops." I have commanded three squadrons in the United States Navy, and it is not difficult to maintain discipline and order when you have a brig or prison for those who disobey, and pay and other rewards for those who do their duties.

In an early revolutionary or counter-revolutionary organization such as you will lead or help to lead, there is, of course, no pay. Our people all over the world work for the sheer love of their race and nations and our holy Cause. Eventually, it is hoped, they will also extend this love to a recognized and trusted Leader.

And it is illegal everywhere for private citizens to imprison people or otherwise apply the sort of legal sanctions imposed by courts, both civil and martial.

The only sort of reward you can offer your followers would be inner satisfaction, praise, commendations, decorations, and the winning of your personal approbation after you have won stature as a "leader." Not many commanders in our military forces could keep even one of their subordinates on duty if all pay and benefits were withdrawn and they had to depend on such idealistic "rewards" to keep their troops together.

And the only sort of punishment you can mete out will be disapprobation, dismissal, and relatively minor extra duties which the follower may or may not be willing to accept voluntarily.

One of the bitter paradoxes of leading such an organization is that the supreme weapon of the leader, dismissal of the offender, actually hurts the leader as much or worse than the offender.

Further, conditions in the early years of an organization such as ours (or any revolutionary or counter-revolutionary organization) are so brutal and hard to take that, inevitably, in spite of the most inspired leadership, there will come many times when almost any member of the group who may have been disciplined, passed over for promotion or otherwise hurt, may be able to gather around him other members who feel a lack of confidence in the leadership strictly because of the hard living conditions or their own weaknesses.

When this happens, you will have a "mutiny." Mutiny is endemic to any organization that, either through faulty leadership or extended periods of setbacks and hardships, subjects the membership to the tremendous psychological hazard of defeatism and rationalization. No military leader alive suffered a series of setbacks and defeats without experiencing some degree of mutiny and/or rebellion from some of his officers or troops who feel they know better or know it all and attempt to hurt or overthrow the leader. In some cases, of course, this is justified. But such cases are extremely rare. No matter how bad a leader may be, mutiny seldom, if ever, helps and almost always hurts by weakening whatever resistance the group can muster against the attacks upon it.

I will go into more detail on handling mutinies, which you will experience as surely as the night follows the day, later in this lesson. For now, suffice to say that a mutiny will be the supreme threat to your personal leadership—your ability to handle men. In a sense, a mutiny is Nature's way of testing a would-be leader in the fires of hard experience. A leader who can be brought down by a mutiny is no leader. And a leader who surmounts and defeats a mutiny, especially if he can succeed in winning back the loyalty of some participants who were merely misled by the real mutineers, will be a far better leader for his experience, with greatly increased stature in the eyes of the troops.

EXPERIENCE AND TRAINING

I will not deny that really great leadership must be born into a person. A sheep can never learn to be a lion. But on the other hand, a lion cannot lead other lions successfully without learning certain lessons of leadership and without experience—including failures.

This lesson is designed to impart to the would-be counter-revolutionary leader the basic techniques and principles of organizing and leading men under rough and combat conditions. A sheep-like man may read it and study it and know it by heart and still be a sheep, unable to lead a bunch of Girl Scouts. But a fighting man, who has any native capacity to lead, will find that the principles enunciated herein will save him years of costly and perhaps fatal errors in leadership which he would otherwise make, finding out for himself what is set forth here. In fact, most of the lessons here are the result of my own personal and often wretchedly miserable stumbling and struggling toward a level of professional leadership which now stands me in good stead and, at least so far, has enabled me to hold together a group of young tigers, to give them a unity and disciplined organization unequaled in the right wing. I will confess, of course, that there is still a tremendous amount to be desired in this direction. But an examination of the history of all revolutionary and counter-revolutionary movements, political and religious, shows that we have made very satisfactory progress in establishing order and discipline at this stage of our operation and with the human material at hand.

PHILOSOPHY OF LEADERSHIP

I think General Patton's explanation of leadership is just about unbeatable. Patton said, "It's impossible to make a piece of string move by getting behind it and pushing. The only way you can move that piece of string is to get up front and pull."

There may be some circumstances in military or civilian life where the reward is so great or the punishment so terrible—or both—that it is possible to lead over a short period of time from the rear—by pushing—by giving "orders."

But in the long run, no leader can survive and lead except UP FRONT.

In a rough and "hairy" combat situation, when a squad of men is pinned down by heavy fire, you will never in a million years get them to make a heroic charge into the teeth of the deadly danger by issuing an order from the safety of the rear. Under such circumstances, it takes a death-defying and heroic type of leadership willing to jump up shouting, "Come on, you sons-of-bitches! Do you want to live forever?" and "CHARGE!" Such leadership carries with it a tremendous risk of personal catastrophe.

Precisely the same principle prevails in the right wing today. In every anti-Communist, pro-White, Christian movement, you find endless voices murmuring and moaning, "What can we do?"

Usually, all these people will do is write letters, make anonymous telephone calls, pass around petitions, go to private meetings, and whisper to each other about the "Eskimos"—meaning Jews. If the future of Western Civilization depends on such pantywaist "soldiers," we will not survive.

The only kind of people who will eventually save our race and nation, if it is to be saved, are the ordinary White working people of the nation whose instincts are still relatively pure and who are not so bourgeois-ized and so yellow that they run like rabbits before the fight even begins at the mere mention of the word. The "ordinary guy" in America WILL FIGHT, but it will take inspired leadership first to organize these inarticulate and brainwashed millions and second to launch them at the throats of the enemy.

Only those who are willing to risk their very lives and their liberty in prison, in addition to the abilities and talents, will be equal to these Herculean tasks of saving White, Western, Christian Civilization.

I cannot emphasize this point too strongly. It is perhaps possible to lead the Boy Scouts, the Birch Society, the Christian Crusade, and even the "Minutemen" from a desk or a "hideout."

It is utterly impossible to lead a counter-revolution against the Communist-nigger-Jew revolution from either a desk or a hideout.

When I am asked, as I always am, "How do you recruit your members?" I always reply that we do not "recruit." We literally make people FIGHT their way into the upper echelons of the Party and into the Party itself.

And we do not issue recruiting folders or beg people to join. We use only one method to gain followers and that is combat and heroism.

When I am asked by a would-be leader, "How can I get a group together in this city?" I always answer, "Put on a uniform and an armband and go down and picket the local office of the Anti-Defamation League or the Communist Party. You will get all of the letters you want from the only kind of people we want addressed to you in jail."

As I have pointed out in a hundred articles, we are not engaged in a battle of ideas as much as the Jews, liberals, and conservatives try to pretend that is the case. Millions of Americans are fed up to the gills with what the Jews, niggers, and Communists are doing, but are simply too disorganized, too inarticulate, and completely unled to be able to do anything about it. No man will ever be able to lead a mass movement who does not first prove that he is a MAN and something of a "hero."

Therefore, the first rule of leadership in this course is to do your best to act in the best traditions of what I call the "heroic manner."

CHARGE! And when you are thrown back, CHARGE AGAIN. There will always be a tiny few who will follow you. And the rest are worthless, nay, a downright drag, in the early stages of a revolutionary or counter-revolutionary movement.

When I say "Charge!", I do not mean simply to go out and commit a felonious assault or otherwise break the law.

At this stage of the fight, when we are almost penniless, pitifully weak, and thoroughly misunderstood by our own people, heroic "attack" consists almost entirely in trying simply to exert your fundamental rights of free speech in the streets.

When you attempt to picket a Jew Communist meeting and expose the Jewish nature of its leaders, or you try to make a speech in public exposing the fact of the Jewishness of Communism and the Jewish leaders of the race-mixing organizations, you will find yourself brutally attacked by the same Jews who preach "academic freedom," "toleration," and "brotherhood."

I have even been beaten over the head with a picket sign reading "Jesus is Love!" on one side and "Love is the Answer!" on the other side—wielded like a club by a yellow-skinned, bug-eyed, liver-lipped Jew-Unitarian-peace-creep.

Just three days ago, as I dictate this, I was able to charge into a mob of several thousand New York "peace creeps" and tear down a Communist, Vietcong flag—without suffering more than temporary jailing and a $10 disorderly conduct fine.

But it took us five years of hell to reach that point.

The only reason I was not charged with all sorts of additional crimes and dragged off to prison was that we have taught the Jews at the top levels that we will give them such a fight that the resulting publicity hurts them more than the jail hurts us. They wanted no part of a public trial with me charged with pulling down a Communist Vietcong enemy flag in front of the Capitol. It would have earned us too much sympathy and exposed them too much.

But before we could reach this point, it is important for you to understand that we had to risk much and suffer much in the way of beatings, jailings, insane asylum incarcerations, etc., for a period of years.

In the early days, whenever we were arrested, the moment the court trial was over, and I was able to be released from jail either on bail or after serving time, I would dash right out on the courthouse steps and give the same speech for which we were arrested in the first place.

Time after time, when we were attacked by mobs, beaten, and then unfairly jailed as criminals, we would lose not one moment in returning to precisely the same point where we were arrested and reassert our Constitutional rights of free speech.

Once the Jews realized that no kind of terror—neither physical nor legal—could stop us, most such attacks stopped. Most police officers understand, respect, and even like us today. But when we started, we represented simply more "trouble," and we "caught it."

Unless you are prepared, personally, to "catch it" yourself, you will never be able to lead the White Man's counter-revolutionary movement against the nigger-Jew mutiny now raging all over the world under the banners of Communism, Zionism, and niggerism.

To wind up this section on gathering followers, let me repeat that you should never "recruit" by pleading with and begging other White men to help you fight. Even if you are successful in gaining converts in this manner, they will be worthless the moment a real fight begins.

In short, the way to win followers is to lead. I started alone over five years ago, and we now have an organization all over the world.

Do not make excuses. No matter who you are, or what you are, if you have basic, minimum intelligence and GUTS, and you know the contents of this course, you can succeed with a unit of your own in your area simply by getting out there and CHARGING!

The first "troops" you will attract will most likely be pretty "wild."

"Respectable" people will be scared to death of you. The only kind of men who will probably be willing to take a chance along with you will be what are usually called "hoodlums." Your job will be to re-direct the aggressive energies of these lads, whose instincts are basically good, and teach them to quit fighting society and the law, which represents it, and direct their attacks at the real enemy, the disloyal Communists, Zionists, and race-mixing traitors who seek to destroy our nation and race.

It is surprisingly easy to do this. Most young men today have never had a real father. They have grown up under a "peace creep," sniveling, democratic, emasculated, and henpecked job-slave, who is currently ridiculed on television, the movies, etc., as a "modern" American "father."

Young men today are surrounded with such sickening "peace creepism" that any red-blooded, old-fashioned American boy is almost forced to become a "delinquent."

Given an example of courageous but responsible leadership, they will quickly follow.

In the FIGHT to save our race and nation, I would a thousand times rather have a young ex-"delinquent" than a thousand of the gutless Beatle-worshipers who could not and would not fight their way out of a wet paper bag.

But the very qualities in the young fighters you will attract which make them worthwhile also make them extremely hard to handle—just as the best horse is the wildest, strongest, and leading stallion, once he is tamed.

The very first rule in leading such courageous, aggressive, and strong men is: Never ask them to do anything you would not do yourself.

If you demand of your men that they perform heroically at your command, you yourself must set an example of even greater heroism. Later, when your group grows, your responsibility will make it difficult to demonstrate your heroism as often as you would like to. You cannot afford to risk long periods of imprisonment or recuperation in a hospital except for the very greatest possible gains for the Party.

Nevertheless, I make it a rule to risk myself in dangerous activity once a year at the very least, with the result that I am arrested and go to jail after the fight or whatever.

I cannot emphasize strongly enough that your continued success as a leader will depend on the conviction in the hearts of all your followers that you are COURAGEOUS—in addition to wise and capable. Cleverness and even genius have nothing to do with winning the love of fighting men. Courage, and courage alone, will win and hold their love, and it is your duty not only to have that courage, but to demonstrate it over and over again.

AUTHORITY

Most young and/or inexperienced leaders try to exert either too much or too little authority in the beginning. Most of the young men I have put in authority here have either tried to be young Napoleons or else they have tried to "grandmother" the men. Either course quickly leads to rebellion and catastrophe.

You should never hesitate an instant to use your authority as a leader to the fullest extent when it is absolutely necessary, but on the other hand, you should try to keep occasions for such necessity to an absolute minimum. You should rarely give a direct order. If you conduct yourself properly as a leader, your suggestion, even in a most subtle and mild manner, will launch your subordinates into instant and enthusiastic action. If this is not the case, then even the most emphatic orders roared at the followers will produce only opposition and rebellion.

Our kind of people hate like hell to be "bossed." They are intelligent enough to realize the necessity for order and discipline, and many of them (including myself) do not find obedience to orders from a competent and courageous superior hard to take, because of their love of order, discipline, and efficiency. Nevertheless, arrogance and officiousness will quickly destroy any would-be leader.

On the other hand, a leader cannot tolerate any form of insubordination or defiance.

In the old British Navy, no crime was punished so viciously and thoroughly as the least sign of defiance of authority—with good reason.

In Nature, there are few things so low and despised as a fallen and beaten leader. Nature casts out and destroys a leader who cannot lead, for the very good reason of the group's survival. For the same reason, you cannot and must not tolerate the slightest OPEN defiance. You should always be very forgiving and understanding of mistakes and sometimes even poor performance by your subordinates. But any sign of defiance, especially before other members of the organization, must bring forth from you MAXIMUM and immediate measures to smash the last shred of such defiance!

In the course of organizing and leading this movement for over six years now, I have experienced literally dozens of mutinies, most of them minor, but three of them large and deadly.

With all of them, large and small, I have dropped everything else and put every ounce of my energy, knowledge, ability, and courage into an all-out attack on the last vestiges of defiance.

It takes only one successful mutiny to destroy all you may have done!

Even if you survive such a mutiny, unless you have succeeded in openly humbling and putting down the mutineers, you will never again be able to command the full loyalty, respect, and obedience of your followers.

This does not mean that you should be vindictive, cruel, or vicious in any manner. The instant a would-be "mutineer" has been "beaten down" and is no longer defiant, you can afford to be as generous as you feel circumstances warrant. Of course, you must publicly penalize such a mutineer in justice to those who were loyal, but there need be no viciousness about it.

All your ferocity and viciousness, however, should be exerted in the fight to destroy and put down the mutiny immediately it occurs.

Often, such mutinies require more courage on your part than action against the enemy. Usually, the mutineers know personal things about you which they threaten to use and expose, etc., and the depths of meanness to which even some of your best friends may go when they are carried away with other mutineers is unbelievable. When such things occur, you must be prepared to risk all and stop at nothing to face up to the "rebels."

Here, as with police departments, I have learned that when the opposition knows you fear absolutely nothing and are ready for any amount of "trouble," they lose their stomach for further action.

ORDERS

Never give an order you do not plan to enforce to the limit.

Almost all military commands and organizations I have been in have made the mistake of issuing hundreds of detailed orders that are posted on bulletin boards and never enforced. This is one of the great curses of modern bureaucratic living, and it absolutely destroys the respect subordinates should have for "ORDERS."

The secret here is to give as few "orders" as humanly possible. Do not try to legislate every tiny facet of existence for your people; let them "muddle through" some things by themselves, even if you think an "order" might make the organization a tiny bit more "efficient." In the long run, orders pertaining to brushing of teeth and similar subjects will be so often violated that your orders will become "toothless."

On the other hand, once you have given an "order," ENFORCE IT!

If it becomes obsolete, rescind it.

Watch your subordinates. If one of them tends to be the overbearing type, who loves to give orders and takes pleasure in officious and arrogant "bossiness," put your foot down immediately, otherwise your own authority will be undermined.

In this same connection, never tolerate one of your subordinates in a position of authority if he is unfit to hold that position. A weakling or a damned fool whom you commission as an officer, or an officious prig who "throws his weight around," will quickly spread among your troops not only a lack of respect for officers and authority, but a positive hatred of your subordinate leaders.

The only cure, when such a misfit "officer" appears, is for you to first try privately to ease such a misfit out of his position of authority. If it cannot be done privately, then you will have no choice but to pull down such a failure PUBLICLY. The purpose of such public humiliation is not sadistic against the offender, but rather a demonstration to the troops that you insist on the highest standards of leadership in your subordinate officers.

There will be another lesson, later on, on "Advanced Leadership," but for the present, let me sum up by repeating the first part of the lesson—you cannot lead from the rear; you must get out in front and show what you want done, not by talking about it, but by doing it YOURSELF!

Further Lessons in LEADERSHIP to follow.

Next Lesson:

FIGHTING YOUR OWN LAW SUITS

LESSON NO. 7
Test Questions

1. What is the most serious kind of disciplinary problem?

2. Why?

3. How should it always be dealt with?

4. Why?

5. Why is it particularly difficult to control right-wing radicals?

6. What are the two standard tools of discipline in most organizations that are lacking in our groups?

7. What is the ultimate penalty available to you as the leader of volunteers and why is it so dangerous to use?

8. Name some of the basic causes of a "mutiny."

9. What two kinds of people make up a group of mutineers?

10. How should you deal with each type?

11. Why are mutinies ALWAYS bad, even when the leader is bad and does not deserve command?

12. What is the supreme test, of a leader's capabilities?

13. Why should mutineers never be allowed to return?

14. Name the FIRST principle of combat leadership.

15. What is the best way to recruit new members?

16. What should you always do when you are falsely arrested and jailed for trying to exert your rights? (after getting out of jail)

17. Why?

18. Can young "hoodlums" be saved?

19. Why,—and how?

20. What causes so many good young men to become delinquents today?

21. In leading courageous men on combat missions, what is the first rule with regard to what you ask them to do?

22. Explain how you should use authority over men.

23. Why is this especially true in dealing with our young counter-revolutionaries?

24. Name the one thing that should <u>always</u> call forth your last ounce of energy and will as a leader.

25. How can you maintain respect for the orders you give?

LESSON NO. 8

Fighting Your Own Lawsuits

Enforcing Your Rights

Did you know that I can come to your house and cart off every stick of furniture—LEGALLY—with a sheriff?

Not one person in a hundred thousand would know what to do.

What would YOU do if you didn't have a lawyer and couldn't pay one if you did?

Or what would you do if you loaned me some valuable books, and I flatly refused to return them, claiming that you "gave" them to me?

What would you do if the police in your area simply arrested you every time you tried to picket, pass out literature, or just walk down the street?

Most people don't have the faintest notion of what they can and cannot do with and within the law, nor do they know what they can do to OTHER people who try to push them around.

Actually, the Communists have developed a devilish technique of USING the letter of the law to hound and drive their opponents sometimes to the point of suicide. They pick some soft, bourgeois citizen who makes a statement that one of the comrades is a "Red," and then sue him with every trick in the book. Their lawyers are tops; they miss nothing, and they WORK. The result is that the victim is forced to pay his own lawyers a fortune just to avoid catastrophe, not to win anything, but just to avoid a judgment which would take everything the victim owns, and garnishee his wages for years to come.

This is a form of legal guerrilla warfare. And the old maxim that attack is the best defense holds true. You have everything to lose and nothing to gain in court fighting the Reds just to hold off a judgment. The only way to save yourself is to COUNTERATTACK!

But you will find more than 90% of lawyers afraid to get mixed up in such "controversial" cases, and the few who are willing to do so charge monstrous fees. And even then, they won't really FIGHT. They eternally counsel caution and timidity. "It won't work" and "It can't be done," I have learned, are their favorite phrases in such cases.

The sad thing about all this is that it is relatively easy to fight this kind of garbage YOURSELF—to ATTACK, using their own methods. But "The Law" scares most people so badly that they never even consider the possibility of anything more than cursing the Jews, Federal Government, Commies, etc., etc.—or possibly of taking out their frustration in some act of senseless violence which merely gives the enemy the pleasure of seeing one of us killed, wounded, and/or imprisoned.

This lesson is designed to give you a working knowledge of enough of the "civil law" to enable you to "stay on your feet" if attacked by the Jews or their lackeys in court, and eventually to enable you to put the fear of God into the creeps by filing and fighting YOUR OWN CASES IN COURT!

For many, this lesson will seem like the toughest one of all to study and absorb. I can't help making at least the first part of it a little dry. But let me assure the student that few things will give him as much satisfaction as going into court one fine day and filing a hell-raising suit against such people as mayors, governors, cabinet officers, etc., when they have overstepped their authority—all of which I have successfully done. These dignitaries howl in agony when one of the "ants" they presumed they could step on suddenly grabs hold of their toe and sinks his fangs into them, which teaches them forever after that Nazis—no matter how small—ain't "ants" who can be stepped on like most other people. Nazis BITE!

What follows will be your legal "teeth" which you can sink into the enemy one day and enjoy his screams of surprise and agony. But, just like getting your regular teeth, the process is sometimes a little painful and requires some "gnawing" to sharpen them. This lesson will require you to work harder than any of the others, but you'll find it well worth the effort.

"THE LAW"

The first thing to learn about "the law" is that it ain't as mysterious and frightening as it appears to most non-lawyers. Just like doctors, lawyers get a certain subconscious "kick" for their ego by all the Latin hocus-pocus which only they can understand. There is also the business of fees; a doctor can get five bucks prescribing "salicylic acid tablets," while he wouldn't get ten cents for calling it "aspirin." A lawyer can get more for a "Writ of Replevin" than he could for a notice to "Turn Loose" of something you own and want back.

But all the Latin technicalities obscure the fundamental fact about the law, which is that LAW IS NOTHING BUT ORGANIZED AND FORMALIZED COMMON-

SENSE.

The layman first coming in contact with the law is usually so overwhelmed with all the technicalities that he cannot see and appreciate the simple and necessary reasons for what certainly APPEAR to be "technicalities."

If YOU, just YOU, could live a thousand years and had to be a judge, YOU would eventually evolve the whole body of what is called "law," because you would HAVE to; it would be the only way you could be "fair."

I will not deny that there are often damned fool technicalities, and that these often pervert and even destroy justice. But my experience has been that there is usually some way around the technicality if you fight hard enough, and eventually, unjust "technicalities" are eliminated.

To use the law effectively, even without an attorney, it is not necessary to know ten million of these "technicalities," or even ten thousand of them; But it is absolutely necessary to know the BASIC PRINCIPLES of the law, and where to find the details and technicalities once you know the general principles under which you must operate.

The first of these basic principles is that there are two KINDS of law—"substantive" and "administrative."

Substantive law is the set of rules by which men have agreed to govern their conduct, the "rules of civilization and business," so to speak.

The substantive law that deals with the rules society has established to protect itself and its citizens from killers, robbers, crooks, etc., is called "criminal law."

The substantive law that protects the orderly and just course of business and the relations between individuals is called the "civil law."

All substantive law is either "common law" or is in the form of specific statutes or, more simply, LAWS.

"Common law" is the set of obvious common-sense rules that make it a crime to commit murder, to steal, rob, defraud, etc. Most modern states and nations, however, have written up the ancient common law into various "codes" consisting of "statutes," or laws.

One of the first things with which you should become familiar is the "code" or set of statutes for your state and city. These govern what you can and cannot do, and how you may do what is permitted.

In addition to criminal statutes, or laws, most states have made up "codes" of statutes dealing with business, community relations, family relations, etc. This is called the CIVIL LAW, and is the main subject matter of this lesson.

CIVIL LAW is generally not involved with jails or other "punishments," except in the case of contempt of an order of a court. The orders of a court take the form of "judgments" or "orders," and these orders, when finalized after all appeals, have the power of life and death over every citizen and whole states.

The METHOD of proceeding in these courts to obtain these judgments for one side or the other is called "administrative law."

In all criminal proceedings, the complaining party is always the "State" or the "people," represented by the "district attorney" or other such officer.

In most (but not all) civil proceedings, the complaining party is an individual or a corporation.

Most of the knowledge of a lawyer that you don't have is this administrative law. You already know it is wrong to murder, cheat, steal, etc. And you know it is wrong for somebody to gyp you. But when you want to go into court or are dragged into court on one of these things, what you DON'T know is the METHOD of proceeding. Usually, you don't even have the faintest notion of WHERE to proceed or how to begin.

It is learning this administrative law, this methodology, that is difficult for most people, but this lesson is to help you do it well enough so you can at least survive in legal proceedings and, one day, launch out and fight your own battles.

There are two main kinds of civil proceedings. The first one is a suit "at law," by which is meant a suit by you against an individual or some corporation for DAMAGES, for MONEY in repayment of damages you have sustained (often called "torts"). If the "remedy" you seek in a court is MONEY, then it is a "lawsuit."

But suppose somebody has contracted to sell you the old log cabin in which you or your father were born and then has welched on the deal, after you paid him some money, and he claims that some other piece of property he tries to fob off on you is "just as good" or even "better." Maybe it is. But you want THAT particular piece of land, and no other. Money won't help you. You want the other guy to do a particular thing, namely, give you possession of the land for which you contracted.

Then you must sue in a "Court of Equity." That name, "Court of Equity," is only a ten-dollar word for "Court of Fairness." When somebody has committed an "inequity" (an "unfairness") against you, you go into the Court of Equity and prove it, and the judge will order the other guy—not to pay money—but to do what is "equitable"—to do what is FAIR.

Often, the "law court" and the "equity court" are the same courtroom and the same judge, but the rules of proceeding are different. You will discover that as you go along.

The only thing you need to understand clearly at this

point is that to enforce your rights to speak, picket and be free from harassment, etc., you go into the CIVIL courts, not the criminal (unless what the authorities have done is a serious criminal violation of your rights, in which case you should first complain to the FBI and then, perhaps, take the matter before a federal grand jury to get the guilty officials indicted).

But when you seek to picket, and the police arrest you every time without cause, or simply run you off, you'll have a hard time making a criminal case against them. You are far better off to go into the CIVIL COURTS and demand a "prohibitory injunction" (an order forbidding the officials to "mess" with you illegally) or a "mandatory injunction" (sometimes called a "writ of mandamus") ordering the officials to DO something positive, such as provide normal protection, for instance.

In organizing and setting up a headquarters, you will need to know the law of contracts, perhaps, more thoroughly than any other single aspect of business law.

The basic principle involved is that the state, the whole people, must ensure that orderly and just business relations between individuals and groups in the community are protected from predatory individuals who would break contracts, fail to pay their debts, and otherwise disrupt the orderly and just course of business.

Therefore, if you have entered into a contract to perform or have somebody perform any legal thing, and the other party fails to perform in any way, you can go into a court of law and demand and get a judgment for "damages" in money or, in a case in equity, for an order commanding the other party to do what he agreed to do or not to do what he agreed not to do.

At this point, it should be carefully noted that the courts cannot and will not enforce the performance of a contract involving an illegal activity or thing, such as, for instance, slavery. Nor can you "sell" yourself into bonded service, as once was done. Whatever is deemed "against public policy" will not be enforced in court, and any money paid under such a contract is gone.

There are certain elements that absolutely must be present in any contract for it to be binding and enforceable in court.

First is the matter of whether it must be in writing or can be verbal.

Verbal contracts, in most cases and in many states, are valid for relatively small amounts and can be performed in less than one year. However, I suggest that in our "business" (which is counter-revolution), the student should avoid verbal contracts wherever it is humanly possible.

Here is a sample of a valid legal contract that will stand up under the acid test of court proceedings:

<u>LEASE AGREEMENT</u>

<u>WITNESSETH:</u> This agreement, entered Into this________day of March, 1965, between John Doe, hereinafter called the Lessor, and Richard Roe, hereinafter called the Lessee, by the terms of which agreement for the sum of One Hundred Dollars ($100.00) paid in advance, receipt of which is hereby acknowledged by the Lessor, Lessee rents from the Lessor. a certain "Harris 22 Offset Duplicator," Serial No. 889, together with all attachments thereto, for a period of five years from the date hereof, at Twenty Dollars ($20.00) rental per year; title to remain with Lessor.

Lessee agrees to insure the said duplicator against fire, theft, and any other reasonable coverage that may be required by Lessor. Lessee agrees to maintain the duplicator in good condition and to be responsible for all repairs and maintenance. Lessee agrees to keep the press at 111 Main Street, and to notify the Lessor in writing if it becomes necessary to move the duplicator to another location.

____
(Lessor)

____
(Lessee)

Date:____________

Subscribed to and sworn to before me by John Doe this________day of March 1965.

____
(Notary Public)

My commission expires:

Note that this contract has been witnessed under oath by a notary public. This is not absolutely necessary to the validation of a contract, but with the cards stacked against us as they usually are, it is far better to bend way over backward, being legal and super-legal. Such attestation by a notary creates a permanent, unanswerable documentary record that the contract was executed at a certain time and placed under oath, and the document cannot be questioned for that reason.

The main element of a good contract is CONSIDERATION.

It is of no validity if you and I sign a contract whereby you "sell" me a car, no matter how carefully the car is described, <u>unless the contract, on its face, clearly sets forth what I gave you for the car—something of value</u>.

Technically and legally, the contract for the sale of a car, for "One Dollar and other valuable considerations," will stand up in court.

But I suggest that our people make no such contracts because it is conceivable that some judge, with our type of cases and the prejudice against us, would declare such a contract to "fail" for "lack of sufficient consideration."

Therefore, make your contracts for genuine and honest consideration of sufficient value to hold up in court. This is a check-off list of the things that MUST be in any contract for anything at all. With this list, you can construct your own contracts, lease agreements, etc., without worrying about "technicalities" as most people do.

Remember that what the law looks for is not the beauty of the writing, the magnificence of the technical language, or the red ribbons sealed on the paper—but rather what is called the "meeting of the minds," a clear indication on the contract that the two parties involved thoroughly understood each other and came to a legal and binding AGREEMENT.

Now, here's the list of the basic elements of any contract:

1. A careful and accurate identification of the parties involved in the agreement. If one or more of the parties have very common names, it is well worthwhile to include their addresses or other identifying details to set them apart from any possible other persons with the same name.

2. The date on which the agreement was entered into. It is not absolutely necessary here, but it is sometimes convenient to include the PLACE where the agreement was reached and signed, especially if a notary public does not witness it for you.

3. THE CONSIDERATION: A statement of what Party "a" is going to give in order to get something else from Party "b." This can be any or all of the following: money, services, agreement NOT to do something, rights, etc.

4. The basic aim of the contract. In a lease, this would mean a careful and accurate description of the property being leased. In a contract for work to be performed, it would accurately describe the services involved, etc.

5. The Terms. A careful, simple, and accurate description of how the consideration is to be paid or given and how the contract is to be performed by the other party, with dates, amounts, and all such information.

6. Special subjects of agreement, such as agreement of one party to cover the other party's property with insurance, to agree to keep it in repair, etc. None of these is legally necessary, but they are usually required by one or both parties to the agreement for the protection of either or both.

7. Signatures, with identification. In some jurisdictions, as a carryover from the old days of sealing wax and family crests, etc., a contract is more binding if, after the signature, the following is inserted: "(SEAL)." In the case of contracts between corporations, states, etc., the actual seal of such organizations is used on the contracts.

The main thing to remember about drawing up contracts for renting headquarters, leasing equipment, etc., is the check-off list I have given above. Do not worry if the language is not "technical" SO LONG AS THE UNDERSTANDING BETWEEN YOU AND THE OTHER PARTY IS CRYSTAL CLEAR.

One of the easiest ways to write a contract that will hold up and avoid struggling with technical difficulties is to write it in the form of a letter from you to the other party, somewhat as follows:

"Dear__________________: This letter, when signed by you, will constitute an agreement between us."

And then just go ahead and set forth what you have agreed.

When the other party signs the original letter and has a copy signed by you, you have a binding and legal contract. (Providing all other elements of the arrangement are legal and proper.)

Let me now give you a tip which will save you a fortune.

Most of the legal papers filed in any court are PUBLIC.

For almost any sort of paper you may want to write, there are probably hundreds of excellent samples in your local courthouse.

Go to the Clerk of the Civil Court, dress nicely, carry a briefcase, and ask politely but firmly to see the file on some cases that you are interested in.

I have found Court Clerks everywhere except Philadelphia, and a few other super-Jew and nigger places will be most helpful and courteous in assisting you.

Once you have found the case almost exactly like your own, you can get hundreds and hundreds of dollars worth of free legal help, which has already been done by the lawyers in the case you are studying.

Needless to say, studying these papers from other cases will be useless if you are not very careful to "weed out" anything that would not "fit" in your own case. In other words, you can't simply slavishly copy the other guy's case and expect to succeed.

But the FORM will be there, and in perfect shape for the particular court in which you must operate. And this latter is important. You can get general forms, as will be shown later, in books in the library, but every court has its peculiar and special rules which you must know to succeed. These can best be found in copies of the court's rules and in other cases in that court. While we are on the subject of courts, let me suggest that, whenever possible, you proceed in the federal courts rather than the state courts.

Except in very fortunate circumstances (which I have here in Virginia), city and state courts are much more likely to give you a "hard time" than the federal courts, for the simple reason that the local judges are much more subject to Jewish, Negro, or Communist and other local pressures than the federal judges who are on the bench for life and are really independent.

All court proceedings start with some sort of a "complaint," even criminal proceedings. In criminal proceedings, the "complaint" consists of an information, an indictment, or simply a charge of a misdemeanor.

In the civil courts, the complaint is literally that—a statement in which the "plaintiff" (the aggrieved party) comes forward to the court, and COMPLAINS. He states the reasons for his complaint as briefly as possible, and then sets forth the "REMEDY" which he asks or demands. Finally, he puts this in the form of a "PRAYER" to the court for the "RELIEF" that he asks, "plus such other reasonable relief as to the court may seem just and proper."

Before you go into court on any kind of proceeding whatever, you should first locate a good law library near you, such as in a law school, in a big public library, or the Bar Association library, where you can often get permission to do some research work.

The first thing to look for in a law library, in researching your case, is a set of books called *Words and Phrases*. In this set of books, you can find almost any word or combination of words that make up the case in which you are involved.

After looking up such subject matter of your case, you will find references under the proper heading to all the various aspects of the law regarding that subject.

In referring to these various books of the law, they use a system of "citations" as follows:

First will come a numeral indicating the volume of a set of books, then an abbreviation for the particular law books in which you can find the case or the law, and next is the page number on which the reference appears. Thus, 19 L. Ed. 24 means the 19th volume of the *Lawyer's Edition*, page 24.

In this lesson, I cannot go into great detail about all the books available, which must be around a million or so, but you can get help from your librarian at first in locating citations until you have become familiar with what is available in your library.

After you have studied the subject in *Words and Phrases*, you should go to one of the two major law "encyclopedias", either *Corpus Juris Secundum* or *American Jurisprudence*.

These two basic law research tools will give you a pretty clear picture of the whole subject about which your case revolves.

It will also cite actual cases in which the same sort of subject has been fought out in court, so you can read just what happened.

When you find the particular facet of the subject, you should actually go and check some of the cases cited in one of these encyclopedias.

You should also look for any textbooks or general readers' books available on the specific subject in which you are interested.

After you have thoroughly researched your case in this manner, and with the help of the librarian, you have tracked down several similar cases, and after you have examined some actual papers of the same nature on the public file in your own area court, you should get one of the books of forms available for filing your complaint.

Since the forms of complaint vary somewhat, especially in state courts, you should try to get the book covering the local area if you are filing a state complaint. If it is a federal complaint, you can go to the Clerk of the Federal Court in your area and purchase a copy of the *Federal Rules of Civil Procedure*. This inexpensive pamphlet gives you detailed rules for proceeding in a federal court, and it's comforting to know that you can operate almost all over the United States with good assurance that compliance with these rules in the federal courts will keep you "in business" in any legal action in these courts.

When you are all set, know the law and the cases it involves, you should file your complaint in the proper court (the federal court if possible), in accordance with the procedures set forth in the manual for the court involved.

There are some things that must be in every complaint, and I will list them here:

First should be the names, identity, and address of the plaintiffs.

Then there should be the same information for the defendants.

Then there should be a title, such as "Complaint for Libel," etc.

The first paragraph of the complaint should establish the JURISDICTION of the court to handle the matter. In federal practice, it is necessary in this paragraph to state the residence or the place of business of both the defendants and the plaintiff, to state that the matter in controversy exceeds $10,000 exclusive of interest and cost, that it involves a federal question of law or constitutional law and/or that there is a "diversity of citizenship"—which means that the plaintiff lives in one state while the defendants live in another and it is therefore impossible for the plaintiff to sue the defendants in his own state since that state cannot serve judicial papers on the citizens of another state.

The second paragraph should set forth the basic facts that constitute your case. There should be no attempt to argue or condemn—merely a rigorously condensed version of the facts which give rise to your complaint.

You will have learned, from your research, what elements of proof are required to sustain the case you file, and you should be sure that you have alleged facts that fulfill all the necessary conditions for getting a judgment in that particular case (for instance, to sustain a judgment for libel, you have to prove that the defendants PUBLISHED the material, that they KNEW it was FALSE, that they did it with MALICE and to expose him to RIDICULE, etc., and that, as a matter of fact, the plaintiff actually did sustain DAMAGES of such and such amount, etc. If any of these allegations are lacking, the case will be thrown out of court on motions of the defendants).

The parenthetical note above brings us to the next subject, the filing of motions before trial.

One of my biggest surprises in learning to struggle through legal cases by myself was the way everybody seems to accept as part of the "game" that the defense will file a whole series of motions, which are almost openly intended to delay and harass as much as possible. I have found everything else about federal practice to be quite reasonable in common sense, except this hanky-panky, which usually delays the case for months and months on end.

As soon as you have filed your complaint, the defense will start filing their harassing and delaying motions, among the first of which is their "Motion to Dismiss the Complaint."

The latter will allege that you have failed to state a claim on which relief can be granted, even though you have claimed that they shot your father and mother, burned your house down, and raped your daughter.

When the shoe is on the other foot, and somebody sues you, this is therefore the first thing to do, before the expiration of the 21-day limit on the summons you will get when served by the other side of the complaint.

Then there is the motion to STRIKE, the complaint as "frivolous," etc., etc. Then, in federal court, there is the right of "Discovery," perhaps the most potent weapon you will have at your disposal.

The theory behind this idea in Federal Courts is that the more matter that is discovered and disposed of out of court, the less the Court's time will be taken up in useless "digging" by opposing sides.

As soon as you have been served with a complaint in a Federal Court, you have the right to send a notice of the taking of a Deposition at any reasonable place you choose, which means that you can ask the opposite parties any reasonable questions UNDER OATH, and they MUST reply, or lose the case, (unless the judge grants them a motion excusing them from the question because it is improper, for one reason or another). I have won several cases in settlements out of Court because the other side COULDN'T answer my honest questions without getting into worse trouble.

When you have filed the suit yourself, you must wait at least 21 days before you can take such depositions.

You can also use "interrogatories," which means you can propound a set of written questions to your adversaries, send them to them with copies to all Parties and the Court, and they must answer, again under oath.

The latter method is much cheaper, of course, since you don't have to pay a court reporter to take everything down and then pay for a transcript. But, on the other hand, there is nothing like personal confrontation, I have found, to catch a liar, especially because you can fire the questions rapidly and the enemy gets no chance to cook up lies which can all hold together, as he can when you send him written questions and he has weeks to think.

After all the preliminary motions and depositions, interrogatories, etc., you will finally get called in for "pre-trial conferences." This means you meet with the judge and the opposition to see if the issues can be narrowed down. In this, it is important to object in writing if anything is done that you feel violates your rights, immunities, etc.

Often, the opposition will demand a bond covering their costs if you are out of the state in which you are suing. I have been thrown out of Court almost solely on this ground by the Jews when I have sued them, since I haven't had the money and couldn't get a bondsman (mostly Jews). But, by the same token, you can turn the tables on them. When YOU are sued, simply demand a bond for costs and watch the other side sweat.

Finally, you will be notified that your case is ready for trial. Gather up all your evidence and witnesses and proceed into the Court Room.

Your conduct of the case in Court will be covered in another complete lesson, later in the course.

Index

www.ingramcontent.com/pod-product-compliance
Lightning Source LLC
LaVergne TN
LVHW082357200926
848481LV00012B/3597